UNIGNORABLE

BURNOUT AND CAREER TRANSITIONS IN NURSING

JEFF RABKIN

CARBONDOG PUBLICATIONS

Agent Contact:

CarbonDog Publications

Menifee, California 92584

carbondogpublications@gmail.com

INTRODUCTION

WHEN THE WORK YOU LOVE STARTS TO COST TOO MUCH

Disclaimer: My wife worked in an ASC for twenty years. Her input was invaluable for this book. Parts of the book may seem to focus on the ASC environment. This was unintended. What's important to remember is that nurses are nurses regardless of where they work. This book is for all nurses seeking change and fulfillment.

$$\sim$$

Most nurses don't wake up one day and decide they're done. Instead, something quieter happens.

You still care. You still show up. You still do your job well. But the work feels heavier than it used to. The patience you once had feels harder to access. You start noticing how much of yourself you leave behind at the end of each shift— and how little is left for the rest of your life. This book is for nurses who recognize that feeling and are trying to understand its meaning.

Burnout is often described as exhaustion, but for nurses, it is rarely just physical. It shows up as emotional depletion, mental fatigue, and a growing sense that the system depends on you without truly supporting you. You may find yourself questioning not whether you are capable, but whether you can keep doing this in the same way.

For hospital nurses, burnout often builds slowly. Long shifts, high acuity, chronic understaffing, and ongoing emotional attachment to patients can make the work feel endless. You carry stories home. You carry responsibility across days and weeks. Even when you rest, your nervous system does not fully stand down.

This book acknowledges something that is rarely said out loud in nursing culture:

It is possible to love nursing and still need to leave clinical practice. That decision does not mean you failed. It does not mean you "couldn't handle it." It means you are paying attention to what your body, your mind, and your life are asking for next.

UNIGNORABLE is a guide for nurses at that crossroads. Inside this book, you will explore:

- How burnout develops differently in hospital and ASC environments
- Practical ways nurses can reduce strain without abandoning professionalism
- What changes—and what doesn't—when moving from a hospital to an ASC
- How to evaluate whether clinical nursing still fits your life

- Realistic pathways out of bedside roles into education, quality, coordination, industry, or non-clinical work

This is not a book about quitting in frustration or pushing through at all costs. It is about making informed, compassionate decisions—grounded in clarity rather than guilt. You are not weak for feeling tired. You are not disloyal for wanting something different. You are not ignorable. You are a nurse responding honestly to the realities of the work. This book exists to help you do that—without shame, without panic, and without losing yourself in the process.

UNDERSTANDING HEALTHCARE DYNAMICS AND YOUR PROFESSIONAL STABILITY

WHY THE RULES HERE FEEL DIFFERENT THAN ANYWHERE ELSE

W alk into any corporate office, and you'll hear people joke about office politics — who took credit for what idea, whose PowerPoint got the loudest applause, who's climbing toward the corner office. Those dramas play out in meeting rooms with smartboards and swivel chairs.

Nursing is a different universe. Here, people entrust their health and lives to the team. Every shift carries meaning. Every role matters. While the culture should reflect that shared importance, the power structure can sometimes lag. Surgeons are often the face of the outcome, which gives them influence that extends beyond the OR doors.

In a typical company, authority comes from titles neatly arranged on an org chart. In an ASC or hospital, the true hierarchy is felt long before it's ever explained. That dynamic isn't inherently wrong — someone must lead. But in healthcare, leadership isn't defined by a corner office. It's defined by how people show up for patients and for one another. In the best centers, the hierarchy supports teamwork. In others, the balance can tilt, and respect becomes uneven. What makes ASCs and hospitals unique is how closely everyone works together. There are no faraway departments, no long chains of command, no buffer zones to hide frustration or miscommunication. In a small team, every strength stands out — and so does every misstep. A single misunderstanding can disrupt the entire day because work is so interconnected. "I didn't know we were using that today." "I thought you said two, not one hour."

Corporate employees discuss "visibility" as a strategy for career growth. In ASCs and hospitals, visibility is inevitable — the question is whether it builds your confidence or challenges it. When communication is clear, roles are respected, and teamwork feels aligned, that visibility becomes a source of pride. It reminds you why you chose this profession. When the environment slips into favoritism or uneven accountability, that same visibility can feel like a spotlight that never turns off. But here's the part worth celebrating: You are part of one of the most important teams in healthcare.

You anticipate a patient's needs before they can articulate them.

You notice what a surgeon needs before they ask.

You ensure that every instrument and every transition is safe.

You didn't choose this career to compete for status. You chose it because you want to provide excellent care, and the ASC gives you the opportunity to do so every day. If corporate life is about moving numbers and messages around, ASC life is about moving people from anxiety to trust — from risk to recovery. That's real impact. That's real responsibility. And you handle it with skill and grace. Yes, there are moments when power dynamics can feel off balance — and we'll talk honestly about those. Recognizing an off-balanced structure around you doesn't make you negative. It makes you strategic. It positions you to communicate confidently, to advocate effectively, and to lead — with or without a title. There are ASCs where teamwork is strong, where respect flows both ways, and where every role is valued. Those places are not fantasy. They are real — and women like you make them real.

Every shift in confidence begins with a change in understanding. When you start paying attention not just to *what* happens in the facility but *why* it happens, the environment becomes easier to understand — and much easier to navigate. You notice differences between days when the team communicates well and days when tension runs unchecked. You observe which surgeons create calm simply by speaking clearly, which administrators take staff concerns seriously, and which coworkers instinctively step in rather than step away when pressure rises. Instead of remembering the shift as simply "good" or "bad," you begin recognizing the behaviors that shape it.

With that awareness comes something even more important: you learn to separate your own worth from the workplace dynamics around you. If a tone turns sharp or a mistake is magnified, you can step back mentally and think, *"This isn't about my value — this is about how communication just broke down."* When disappointment or frustration rises in the room, you learn to see the *system* as the source of the tension, not your personal abilities. Naming the problem correctly preserves confidence.

You also develop a clearer understanding of how influence works within the facility. On paper, the chain of command might look simple — a director here, a manager there — but true decision-making power often runs through trust, consistency, and relationships. You see who people turn to when they need help, whose input surgeons actually consider, and who quietly keeps the center from spinning off its axis. Once you understand those currents of influence, you can position yourself within them instead of feeling pulled around by them.

This new understanding changes how you communicate. Instead of waiting to speak until you're frustrated, you begin choosing your words intentionally. You learn when a surgeon needs a direct, efficient update and when a colleague needs reassurance more than instruction. You realize that being assertive doesn't mean being confrontational — it means being anchored. You can walk into a conversation not to argue, but to align. Not to point out problems, but to show a pathway toward a safer or smoother process. Leadership begins to see that difference. They stop hearing complaints and start hearing solutions — and that shift earns respect.

With this awareness, you stop shrinking yourself to keep the peace. Instead, you grow into a version of yourself that cares deeply *and* speaks confidently. You become someone who understands the rules of the room, not to survive them, but to work skillfully within them. You see exactly which actions elevate teamwork and which undermine it, and you choose — consistently — to be a source of poise, not pressure.

That is how power begins to move toward you. It doesn't require a title. It doesn't need permission. It doesn't even require anyone else to change. It begins when you see the environment clearly enough to stop questioning yourself and start guiding the room by example. You're no longer reacting. You're leading. Even if you're not trying to lead anything or change anything — even if you just want to show up, do your job well, and go home — understanding the dynamics in your facility still matters. Whether you pay attention to them or not, they shape your day. You might not think of yourself as someone navigating politics or managing personalities, but those things still affect how you feel from the moment you clock in to the moment you leave the parking lot. The hierarchy, the communication styles, the subtle power plays — they influence your workload, your stress level, and how confidently you move through each case.

This kind of awareness doesn't happen all at once. It starts the moment you allow yourself to observe the environment with curiosity rather than pressure. Instead of assuming every tense moment is your fault or your responsibility to fix, you begin watching what's happening around you the same way you assess a patient: calmly, attentively, gathering information before drawing conclusions. You notice the difference between a surgeon who is genuinely concerned about a complication and a surgeon who is venting frustration that has nothing to do with you. You see, when a coworker's impatience is due to stress from being short-staffed or running behind. Instead of immediately wondering, *"What did I do wrong?"* you pause and think, *"What's happening in the room right now?"* That slight pause is where confidence begins to grow. You also become more aware of patterns. You see how smoothly everything flows when communication is respectful, when people make space for each other's expertise, when someone cracks a quick joke that resets the tone. You begin to recognize who brings calm and understanding to the room and who tends to stir things up. You see that some people command influence not through authority but through trust — they're the ones others look toward when pressure spikes.

Once you understand those dynamics, you can move through the day with more intention. You know which individuals help the team regroup after a stressful turnover. You know who can quietly back you up if a surgeon challenges a safety decision. You know when the best approach is a direct, concise statement — and when the situation calls for empathy and reassurance. You're no longer guessing how to speak or who to speak to; you're aligned with the rhythm of the work. There's a relief that comes with that. You stop internalizing every raised voice, every hurried demand, every stressful moment. You stop letting the day's mood determine your self-worth. You can see the system clearly enough to understand where you stand in it — and why your role matters. And when you trust your place in the environment instead of trying to survive it, your confidence becomes steadier. You can focus on your job — the care, the safety, the humanity — without feeling responsible for everyone else's reactions. It's not about changing your personality or becoming someone you're not. It's about shifting from *absorbing* the stress around you to *observing* it—and then choosing how to respond with purpose rather than fear. That's when your day feels different. That's when you feel different.

You already carry enough responsibility —patient care, patient safety, and patient comfort. You don't need to carry unspoken anxiety about how the room will react to you. You don't need to leave work replaying every interaction in your head. You don't need to shoulder guilt that doesn't belong to you. When you clearly see the dynamics, you can separate your identity from the environment you work in. You can clock out feeling proud of the care you provided — not weighed down by the room's mood. You don't have to chase leadership roles or fight for influence. You don't have to be the one "changing the culture." You get to enjoy your job more fully — with respect, confidence, and peace.

STEP-BY-STEP PLAN: HOW YOU START SEEING CLEARLY

(And Stop Taking Everything Personally)

1. Decide you're going to be an observer for one week

For the next 5–7 shifts, your only "extra" job is to notice how the place runs. Not to fix it. Not to call anything out. Just observe.

Ask yourself during the day:

- What does it feel like on good days vs bad days?
- What *specifically* is different? (tone, pacing, staffing, certain people present, etc.)

At the end of each shift, jot a few quick notes in your phone or a small notebook. Nothing fancy, just:

"Today felt calmer — Dr. X was here, charge nurse Y communicated clearly, turnover wasn't rushed."

"Today felt chaotic — short-staffed, surgeon snapping, no one calling out the plan."

You're collecting data, not judging yourself.

2. Start naming what makes the environment *healthy*

After a few shifts, look back at your notes and ask:
"When the day goes well, what's happening?"
You'll start to see patterns:

- Is it a particular surgeon who stays respectful under pressure?
- A charge nurse who gives clear direction?
- A tech who keeps everyone laughing without undermining focus?
- An administrator who jumps in instead of disappearing?

Write down 3–5 things that seem to make things better. Those are your "green flags."

3. Name what consistently *undermines* the day
Now do the same thing for rough days:
"When things go sideways, what keeps showing up?"
You might notice:

- The same person is always blaming instead of problem-solving
- Constant schedule changes with no communication
- One surgeon who raises the temperature in every room
- Gossip or eye-rolling that shuts people down

Write down 3–5 things that keep showing up when the day feels heavy. Those are your "red flags."

You've done something powerful: You've moved from "I had a bad day" to "These specific behaviors and dynamics make days harder." That alone takes a lot of weight off you.

4. Map the *real* power and calm in your ASC

Next, take a piece of paper and literally draw three little lists:

- People who **actually make decisions** (formal authority)
- People others naturally **go to for help** (informal authority)
- People who **calm the room down** when they walk in (emotional authority)

You'll quickly see that "who has influence" is not always the same as "who has the title." This matters because if you want support, change, or backup… these are the people you'll go to first.

5. Practice *pausing* instead of *absorbing*

The next time someone snaps, sighs, or gets sharp with you, try a small mental experiment:

Instead of immediately thinking, "What did I do wrong?"

Practice thinking, "What's going on with *them*?" Use this pause to pose a question to them. Questions immediately refocus attention on them and prompt an explanation.

You're not excusing bad behavior. You're just not letting it drill straight into your self-worth.

You might realize:

- They're behind schedule
- They're under pressure from the admin
- They're worried about a complex patient
- It's about them, not you

You can still decide later if the behavior crossed a line. But in the moment, you've given yourself a little emotional buffer. That's huge.

6. Pick one "go-to" support person

From your power/calm map, choose one person you trust who:

- Thinks clearly under pressure, and
- Treats people decently

Make a decision:

"When things feel off, or I'm doubting myself, I'll check in with *this* person."

That might look like:

"Hey, did that interaction seem off to you, too?"

"Was I unclear, or was he just stressed?"

This keeps you anchored in reality rather than spiraling in your thoughts.

7. Experiment with intentional communication

For the next week, choose **one** small way you'll communicate more intentionally.

For example:

- With surgeons who like brevity → give a short, clear statement:

"We're ready to go."

- With coworkers under stress → add a quick human line:

"We're slammed, but we've got this. I can help with the next case."

You're not changing your whole personality. You're just testing which tone and phrasing seem to move everyone in a better direction.

8. Debrief with yourself for 3 minutes after each shift
Before you leave or once you're in your car, ask yourself:

1. What worked better for me today?
2. What felt less personal once I saw the pattern?
3. Where did I handle something with more intention instead of an automatic reaction?
4. DON'T rehash your argument with a co-worker.

You don't need a long journal—just a few sentences. Over time, you'll notice:

- You bounce back faster from tense moments
- You question yourself less
- You feel a little steadier and a little less at the mercy of the day

9. Let this be enough (for now)
You don't have to "fix the culture." You don't have to "be a leader" if you don't want to. This plan is about protecting your confidence and your peace while you do the job you're already good at. Seeing the environment clearly, knowing who has what kind of influence, and responding with greater intention equals you feeling less overwhelmed by every shift and more grounded in who you are. That's the whole point.

Here's an interesting story about power dynamics. I have a friend, Mary, who is a nurse at a large ASC. Her supervisor, Jane, in addition to other responsibilities, managed the schedule. Scheduling was never an issue until the holiday season rolled around. Jane would always wait until the very last moment to notify her staff when she was taking time off. This made it difficult for everybody else to schedule their time off. It was an obvious power play by Jane and completely unnecessary. I told Mary she should complain to "management," but she was afraid of speaking up. Nobody was willing to speak up either. Here is what I have to say about that:

Example Response

Mary doesn't call Jane out. She doesn't accuse her of withholding the schedule. She doesn't go over her head. Instead, she approaches it as an operational improvement.

"Hey Jane, I've noticed our holiday schedule gets finalized close to the actual dates. I understand how busy this time of year is, but it makes it difficult for all of us to plan our availability and ensure we stay fully staffed. Would it be possible to set a standard date each year for releasing the holiday schedule? Something like early November? I think it would help the whole team plan and avoid last-minute staffing gaps."

Then she stops talking—no nervous rambling. No apologizing. A modest suggestion tied directly to staffing stability and patient care. If Jane brushes it off or gives a vague answer, Mary can follow up later with a short email:

"Thanks for considering the earlier release date for the holiday schedule. I think it will really help us plan staffing more effectively."

That email is not confrontational. It simply shows professionalism and creates a quiet record. Mary hasn't "gone over her boss's head." She hasn't attacked anyone. She hasn't created conflict.

She has:

✓ protected her own boundaries

✓ addressed the issue respectfully

✓ framed it as beneficial to the whole ASC

✓ maintained her professionalism

And she has done it in a way that **even a controlling supervisor can't reasonably object to**. If leadership ignores it? That tells Mary something important about the culture—without her ever having taken a risky step. Mary is not alone in this. Her co-workers have the same issue. Here's how a group should address the situation:

Group Suggestion Version (Safe, Subtle, and Effective)

Instead of one nurse making the suggestion and feeling exposed, two or three nurses each raise the same idea in their own words at different times, without referencing one another.

This signals to leadership that the issue affects the *whole* staff, not just a single person.

Here's how that works:

Nurse #1's Approach

A simple, casual, non-emotional mention during an everyday conversation:

"I was thinking—if we had the holiday schedule a little earlier this year, it might help us all plan our time off more smoothly. It could also keep us from scrambling to find last-minute coverage. Would it be possible to release it earlier next time?"

She doesn't sound upset.

She's not complaining.

She's proposing a *helpful improvement.*

Nurse #2's Approach

A day or two later, in a totally separate interaction:

"I've noticed the late holiday schedule creates a rush for everyone. If we posted it earlier, I think it would help us remain fully staffed and reduce last-minute trading. Just something to consider for this season."

No reference to Nurse #1, no coordination implied.

Nurse #3's Approach

Even later, perhaps in passing or during a staff conversation with Jane or a manager:

"We've been talking about ways to make the holiday season smoother. One thing that might help is having the schedule out earlier. It would give everyone breathing room —and make sure we're fully covered for all cases."

Still calm. Still solution-focused. Still safe.

Why This Works So Well

When leadership hears the *same idea* from multiple people—even phrased differently—it no longer sounds like personal frustration. It sounds like:

- a workflow improvement
- a staffing need
- a patient-care safeguard
- a consistent pain point
- something worth fixing

It removes fear for any individual, because **no one stands out as the "complainer."**

Instead, leadership sees a quiet consensus forming. In small ASCs, this is often the most effective and least risky path to change.

Optional Follow-Up (Gentle Nudge)

If leadership still doesn't act, one nurse can email a neutral follow-up:

"Just circling back on the idea of an earlier holiday schedule posting. I think it would really help with planning and ensuring full staffing. If we can try it this year, I'm confident it would support smoother operations."

Again—no pressure, no accusation, no drama.

When I was twelve, my parents sent me to a summer camp. I'm pretty sure my going away for the summer was more for them than for me. The camp was set up with cabins that each held about 16 kids. The cabins were occupied by age. Each cabin had an adult "counselor." I was in cabin six. We were scheduled to go on a three-day camping trip one week, and before we got on the bus, our counselor said, "I don't want to hear any complaining on this trip. If you complain, you're going to bite off a corner of the soap bar. That was the preferred method of punishment at the time. All the counselors ensured their cabins were well-stocked with soap.

Well, guess who got caught complaining before the sleeping bags were rolled out? Yep, it was yours truly, and I was promptly presented with a bar of soap, which I had to bite off a piece in front of everybody, chew for five seconds, and spit out. After that, I stopped complaining outright and looked for ways to phrase my issues without making them sound like complaints. Instead of saying, "I don't want to eat that for dinner," I would say, "What do you guys think about having Mac and cheese instead of spaghetti?" Throughout the trip, I phrased my issues by bringing my fellow campers in on them. It's the nail that stands up that gets pounded down—safety in numbers.

2

GASLIGHTING IN SCRUBS

WHEN YOUR EXPERIENCE IS REAL, BUT THE
ENVIRONMENT MAKES YOU QUESTION IT

G aslighting is a word people usually associate with toxic relationships or manipulative partners, not healthcare settings filled with professionals. But in an ASC, gaslighting rarely looks dramatic or intentional. It's subtle. It's quiet. It often comes wrapped in the language of efficiency, humor, or clinical authority. And most of the time, the person doing it has no idea that's what they're doing. Gaslighting in surgery isn't about grand manipulation. It's about dismissing your reality until you start doubting your own instincts. That doubt is the part that hurts — not because you're weak, but because you care deeply about doing your job right.

You see something.

You hear something.

You clarify something.

You raise a concern.

And instead of collaboration, you're told — directly or indirectly — that what you observed doesn't matter. Or didn't happen. Or shouldn't bother you. Or "isn't this the way things are done here?" Your experience gets quietly overwritten by someone else's authority. Not because you're wrong. But because they're louder, faster, or more senior. And once that happens enough times, the shift doesn't just happen in the room — it happens inside you.

How Gaslighting Shows Up in the ASC (Without Feeling Like Gaslighting)

It rarely sounds like, "You're imagining things." It sounds more like:

"Relax, that's not a big deal."

"That's just how Dr. ___ is."

"We don't need to document that — it'll only make things messy."

"You're overthinking it."

"That didn't happen the way you remember."

"No one else had an issue with that."

"You're being too sensitive; we were just joking."

The message underneath is always the same:

"Your perception is less valid than mine."

In a high-pressure environment where confidence should be your anchor, comments like these tug at your footing. Slowly, quietly, you begin to wonder:

Did I misread that?

Maybe I should just let things go.

Maybe I shouldn't speak up next time.

Maybe I'm the one making this more complicated."

That's the most dangerous part — not the comment itself, but the way it rearranges your belief in yourself.

WHY GASLIGHTING HAPPENS MORE IN Healthcare

It's not because people are cruel. It's because people are rushed, stressed, and conditioned to keep moving.

When a surgeon is behind schedule, it's easier for them to

say, "You must have misheard me," than to revisit a forgotten instruction. When a supervisor feels overwhelmed, it's easier to dismiss a concern than address it. When a colleague makes a mistake, it's easier for them to deflect than take accountability.

Gaslighting often comes from:

- a desire to avoid delay
- a habit of defending the ego
- a misinterpretation of confidence as a challenge
- a belief that efficiency is more important than communication
- a culture that protects revenue over emotional safety

But none of that means you're imagining things. It just means the environment hasn't been trained to support understanding. And that's precisely why your awareness matters.

What Gaslighting Does to a Nurse Who Just Wants to Do Her Job

It makes you second-guess your instincts — the very instincts that keep patients safe.

You begin replaying conversations.

You hesitate before speaking up.

You apologize for things you didn't do.

You feel responsible for tone shifts you didn't cause.

You shrink your presence in the room without even noticing.

Not because you're insecure. But because your confidence has been slowly eroded. No one tells you this part: Gaslighting doesn't damage your knowledge — it damages your trust in your understanding. In a clinical environment, that trust is essential.

How You Start Regaining Your Reality

When you understand that gaslighting in the facility is usually unintentional and driven by pressure, something powerful happens: you stop internalizing it. You begin to see the pattern instead of feeling the sting. You start to distinguish between someone questioning your perception and someone who is overwhelmed and reacting automatically. That understanding removes the emotional charge from the moment. You don't crumble; you observe.

You don't think, *"I'm wrong."*

You think, *"This is a pattern of dismissal I've seen before. It's not about me."*

And once you name it, you stop absorbing it.

Your voice becomes steadier.

Your confidence returns.

Your decisions feel grounded again.

Your reality stays yours.

WHY CALLING It Out Isn't Always Necessary — or Smart

In an ASC, confrontation isn't always the best tool. You're not trying to expose anyone or create tension. You're trying to protect your professional understanding. Gaslighting loses its power not when you attack it, but when you **stop believing it**. That shift is internal — calm, subtle, steady.

It sounds like:

"I know what I saw."

"I know what I heard."

"I know my skill."

"I trust my judgment."

You become the person who can hold her reality even when someone else tries to rewrite it. And that's how gaslighting stops working — without drama, without conflict, and without risking your job.

GASLIGHTING MITIGATION PLAN

Even the most skilled nurses can begin to doubt themselves when someone rewrites a conversation, minimizes a concern, or questions something they clearly saw. Gaslighting in a fast ASC environment is usually subtle, usually unintentional, and almost always tied to pressure. But you can protect your understanding — and your confidence — with a few grounded, practical habits.

Here's how to start.

1. Recognize the moment it's happening

When someone brushes off your concern or suggests you misunderstood something you know you heard, pause and acknowledge it silently:

"This is them reacting. My perception is still valid."

Naming it—even just in your mind—keeps you anchored in your own reality.

2. Calmly restate what *you* understood

You don't need to argue. Just bring the conversation back to the facts:

"Just to clarify, what I heard was…"

"My understanding of your request is…"

You're not challenging their authority.

You're simply putting your reality back on the table.

3. Repeat key information to secure it

When things feel slippery, repeat the plan in the moment:

"So we're confirming X, and not doing Y — Yes?"

This creates understanding, and understanding is something gaslighting can't override.

4. Document neutrally — not emotionally

A neutral note or follow-up message protects you without escalating anything:

"Per our discussion at 10:15, the plan is to proceed with ___. Please let me know if anything changes."

You're not accusing.

You're creating professional understanding.

No reasonable leader can object to that.

5. Check in with someone you trust

A quick reality check can keep you grounded:

"Is this how you understood that conversation?"

"Did that interaction seem off to you, too?"

Sometimes the difference between spiraling and staying steady is a single validating sentence from someone who saw the same thing you did.

6. Separate their tone from the truth

Someone can be stressed, rushed, or mad — and still be wrong about the facts. Their tone reflects their pressure, not your competence. Remind yourself:

"Their stress is theirs. The facts are still the facts."

This is one of the quickest ways to protect your confidence.

7. Have one steady phrase ready

When the conversation feels slippery, a pre-chosen phrase keeps your footing:

"You may remember it differently — this is what I experienced."

"I'm comfortable with what I observed."

You're not escalating.

You're holding your ground without heat.

8. Decide what matters and what doesn't

Not every dismissive moment is worth pursuing. Ask yourself:

- Is this a safety issue?
- Is this a pattern?
- Will addressing it protect my peace or my license?

If the answer is yes, it's worth documenting or a neutral follow-up.

If the answer is no, let your internal understanding be enough. Pick your battles

9. End your shift by anchoring your own reality

Before you go home, take a breath and remind yourself:

"This is what I did well today.

This is what I know I got right.

This is the understanding I'm taking home."

Gaslighting thrives in uncertainty. Your job is not to eliminate the behavior —it's to eliminate its effect on *you*. This plan doesn't require confrontation. It doesn't require calling anyone out. It simply builds a steady internal foundation so your confidence stays intact, no matter what kind of personalities or pressures show up in the room. You don't overcome gaslighting by fighting harder. You overcome it by staying anchored in the truth you already hold.

THE BLAME GAME

WHY RESPONSIBILITY SLIDES DOWNHILL — AND HOW TO STOP CARRYING WHAT ISN'T YOURS

Blame behaves differently in an ASC than in almost any other workplace. In most corporate environments, blame is tangled in emails, meetings, and performance reviews. In surgery, blame moves at the speed of the day. It shows up in tone, in rushed words, in sideways comments made while everyone is trying to keep the schedule on track. Nobody plans to blame anyone. It just happens — fast, reflexively, and often unfairly.

That's because ASCs are high-pressure environments where things must run smoothly to keep both the patients and the schedule safe. When something disrupts that rhythm — a turnover delay, a missing instrument, a miscommunication about a case — everyone feels it immediately. When pressure rises, people seek the quickest possible explanation for *why*. Unfortunately, the fastest explanation is often the wrong one. And the nearest person is often the safest target. Not emotionally safe — *politically* safe.

Surgeons rarely blame anesthesia. Anesthesia rarely blames surgeons. Managers rarely blame owners. Everyone avoids blaming upward. So the weight of frustration rolls downhill, gathering speed until it lands in the hands of the people who had the least control over the situation in the first place: the nurses and techs who are just trying to get the next patient ready. This is why ASC blame feels so personal — because in a small team, it is. But here's a fact, no one says out loud: Blame is seldom about the person being blamed. It's about pressure, pride, and the instinct to protect one's own position in the moment. It's more about venting.

When a surgeon snaps about turnover time, the issue usually isn't you — it's their clinic schedule, or an internal pressure you're not privy to. When a supervisor redirects responsibility toward you, it might not be about your performance — it may be the easiest way for them to avoid taking heat from above. When a coworker deflects a mistake toward you, it might be fear, embarrassment, or habit. None of those things excuses the behavior. But all of them explain why the blame came your way. And when you understand the *why*, you stop assuming the blame is a reflection of your worth or competence.

Why Nurses Absorb Blame More Than Anyone Else

Nurses become the default targets for a simple reason: you are the link between every part of the surgical process. You're the connective tissue of the ASC.

You are in the OR.

You are in pre-op.

You are in PACU.

You answer to management.

You support surgeons.

You guide patients.

That makes you essential — but it also makes you visible. And in moments of stress, visible becomes vulnerable. People blame the person they can reach, rather than the underlying cause. And in most cases, the real cause is systemic:

- A poorly designed workflow
- An unrealistic schedule
- Inadequate staffing
- Missing equipment
- Conflicting expectations between departments
- Mixed messages from leadership

Those aren't "nurse problems." But they often fall onto nurses' shoulders because you're the constant. The one who holds everything together quietly. And the one who absorbs the pressure without wanting to make a scene.

How Blame Affects You (Even When You Know It Isn't Fair)

Even if you know logically that the blame isn't yours, it still lands in your mind:

You replay conversations in your head.

You wonder if you could have done something differently.

You question your professionalism.

You carry the weight home.

That's because blame strikes at your identity. You're in healthcare because you care. You want to do your job well. You want to protect your patients. You want to support the team. So when someone, even briefly, suggests that you're the problem, it's almost impossible not to internalize it. But here's where your power begins: you don't have to absorb blame to be a responsible, conscientious nurse.

You can hear it.

You can evaluate it.

And you can release what isn't yours.

How to Protect Yourself Without Becoming Defensive

The most effective nurses aren't the ones who never face blame — they're the ones who know how to move through it without losing their confidence. The shift begins with understanding. When someone directs blame toward you, pause internally and ask: "Is this about the facts, or about the pressure of the moment?" More often than not, it's pressure.

Then ask yourself:

"If someone else were in my shoes today, would this blame still be happening?" If the answer is yes, the issue is systemic. This simple mental habit frees you from the instinct to personalize every frustrated comment or rushed remark. It lets you respond calmly and professionally:

"Here's what happened from my perspective."

"This is the information I had at the time."

"Let's clarify the process so this doesn't happen again."

Notice the tone:

Not defensive.

Not apologetic.

Not confrontational.

Just steady. Blame thrives when you shrink under it. It dissolves when you meet it with calm understanding.

Why Calm Understanding is Your Best Defense

In a surgical environment, raised voices are normal. But calm is rare — and powerful. When you respond clearly and without fear, something shifts in the room.

People listen differently.

People recalibrate.

People recognize your professionalism.

A nurse who maintains a calm, understanding demeanor becomes someone the team respects—not because she fights, but because she stands up. You don't need to win every disagreement. You need to know that the blame doesn't define you. That internal steadiness is what eventually transforms your external experience. Take a breath and count to five.

BLAME REDIRECT PLAN: STEP-BY-STEP

Step 1: Pause before you react

When someone fires blame at you — *"We're behind because of nursing," "This delay is on you," "Why wasn't this ready?"* — your body reacts first. You feel that jolt of heat in your chest or stomach. Instead of answering from that feeling, give yourself half a second to breathe and think:

"Okay. Don't absorb this yet. Just get clear."

That tiny pause keeps you from snapping back or over-apologizing.

Step 2: Ask yourself, "What actually happened?"

In your head, quickly rewind:

- What time did things really occur?
- What information did you have?
- What was outside your control?

You're not looking for someone to blame — you're pulling up the **facts** so you can stand on them.

Step 3: Lead with a calm, factual statement

Now, instead of defending your character, describe the situation:

- "The previous case ended at 10:05, and anesthesia needed extra time. We started turnover as soon as they were finished."
- "The instrument set arrived in the room at 09:12; we began setup immediately after that."
- "I hadn't been informed of the add-on case until 14:30. Once I knew, I adjusted my assignments."

Short. Steady. Factual. You're not arguing — you're clarifying.

Step 4: Keep your tone low and even

How you say it matters as much as what you say. You don't need to sound angry or wounded. Aim for calm, professional, "report mode" — the same voice you'd use giving a patient update:

"Here's what happened from my side…"

A calm tone signals:

"I am not rattled. I am not fighting you. I am simply bringing the full picture."

Step 5: If needed, widen the lens to the process, not the person

If the blame keeps coming, gently shift the focus from *you* to *the process*:

- "It seems like the delay is coming from how the schedule changes are communicated. We might need a clearer system for that."
- "The turnover time is tight with our current staffing. We may need to look at that if we want to hit these targets consistently."

Now it's not "you versus them." It's "all of us looking at the system."

Step 6: Decide what to document

After a moment like that, ask yourself:

"Is this something future-me might need a record of?"

If yes, make a neutral note or send a brief follow-up:

- "Per our discussion at 10:15, the delay was related to instrument availability; setup began as soon as the tray arrived."

No emotion. No accusation. Just reality on record.

Step 7: Don't take home what isn't yours

At the end of the shift, remind yourself:

- What did I actually control today?
- What did I handle well?
- What wasn't mine to carry?

Blame tries to follow you home. You determine where it stops. "I did my job. I stood in the facts. I'm not bringing someone else's pressure into my evening."

Phrases That Sound Defensive — and the Better Versions to Use Instead

Blame moments can make anyone tighten up. The problem isn't the feeling — it's that certain phrases accidentally make you sound guilty, stressed, or unsure, even when you've done nothing wrong.

Here are the most common defensive responses nurses give, paired with stronger, calmer alternatives.

1. Defensive:

"That wasn't my fault."

Better:

"Here's what happened on my end."

Why it works:

You redirect from blame to understanding without sounding combative.

2. Defensive:

"No one told me!"

Better:

"The information I received was ___, and I acted based on that."

Why it works:

Shows professionalism and protects your credibility.

3. Defensive:

"I was waiting on someone else."

Better:

"We were able to move forward once ___ was completed."

Why it works:

Keeps the focus on workflow, not finger-pointing.

4. Defensive:

"You said to do it that way!"

Better:

"My understanding from our earlier conversation was ___."

Why it works:

Centers on your interpretation, not an accusation.

5. Defensive:

"That's not what happened!"

Better:

"Let me share the sequence of events from my perspective."

Why it works:

Invites discussion instead of a fight.

6. Defensive:

"I didn't do anything wrong."
Better:
"Here's how I approached the situation."
Why it works:
You stay confident without sounding self-protective.
7. Defensive:
"I thought you said…"
Better:
"For understanding, what I heard was ___."
Why it works:
Clarifies without sounding uncertain or flustered.
8. Defensive:
"Well, I wasn't the only one involved."
Better:
"There were several moving parts — here's what I managed on my end."
Why it works:
Acknowledges complexity without shifting blame.
9. Defensive:
"I don't know why that happened."
Better:
"Here's what I saw, and here's what I can confirm."
Why it works:
Shows control of your lane, even if you don't have all the answers.
10. Defensive:
"That's not fair."
Better:
"Let's walk through what occurred so we can pinpoint the issue."
Why it works:
Moves the conversation from emotion to resolution.
The Psychology Behind These Upgrades

Each "better" phrase does three subtle things at once:

1. Shifts the tone from reactive → steady
2. Brings the conversation back to facts instead of feelings
3. Protects your credibility without inviting conflict

This is how you come across as confident, competent, and unshakeable — even when someone is trying to hand blame to you.

BURNOUT

WHEN YOU REALIZE YOU'RE RUNNING ON EMPTY

Burnout rarely announces itself loudly. There's no single moment where everything falls apart. Instead, it slips in quietly, disguised as "just a rough week" or "a busy stretch" or "once things slow down, I'll feel better." Nurses are especially good at explaining it away because caring, endurance, and professionalism have always been part of the job.

At first, you notice that your patience is thinner than it used to be. Minor interruptions irritate you. Conversations that once felt manageable now feel exhausting. You start counting the hours until your shift ends — not because you don't care, but because you're tired in a way sleep doesn't fix.

For hospital nurses, it often feels like a slow erosion. You carry patients longer. You carry patients emotionally over time. In a hospital, you don't just meet a patient and hand them off an hour later. You may care for the same patient for days or weeks. You watch their condition improve, stall, or deteriorate. You learn their family dynamics. You absorb their fear, hope, frustration, and grief.

Even when you go home, parts of those patients stay with you:

- You wonder if they made it through the night
- You replay difficult conversations with families
- You think about the patient who reminded you of your parent, your child, or yourself

That emotional continuity builds attachment — and attachment requires energy. You carry responsibility beyond the moment. Hospital nursing involves ongoing commitment, not task completion. You don't just complete a procedure and move on. You monitor trends, anticipate declines, repeatedly advocate, and escalate concerns that may take days to be addressed.

You hold mental lists:

- "If labs come back like this, I need to call."
- "If their breathing changes, this needs to happen."
- "If staffing drops again tonight, how do I keep them safe?"

That constant mental vigilance doesn't shut off at shift

change — it lingers. You carry moral weight. Hospital nurses often know exactly what good care would look like — and exactly why it isn't happening.

You carry:

- The discomfort of unsafe ratios
- The frustration of delayed orders
- The pain of watching families struggle
- The guilt of not having enough time

Even when none of it is your fault, your conscience stays engaged. That's moral load, not physical work. You carry unresolved outcomes. In an ASC, outcomes are usually clear and immediate. In a hospital, outcomes are uncertain and ongoing.

You may never know how a patient's story ends. You may leave mid-crisis. You may hand off someone who is declining. That lack of closure weighs on the nervous system. Why does this matter?

Carrying patients longer means:

- Your emotional labor compounds
- Recovery takes longer
- Rest doesn't fully reset you
- Burnout builds quietly

It's not about being "too sensitive." It's about sustained exposure to responsibility and humanity without adequate release. You absorb grief, trauma, and moral distress shift after shift. You work short-staffed and do your best to make it look seamless, even when you know the care you're providing isn't the care you'd want for your own family. The charting piles up. The policies keep changing. And over time, the emotional weight of "never enough" settles into your body.

For nurses working in ASC's, it tends to arrive differently. It's sharper and faster. The pace never lets up—Turnovers stack. Expectations stay high. There's little room to pause, regroup, or process anything before the next patient is already rolling in. You stay hyper-focused for hours at a time, managing efficiency, safety, personalities, and precision all at once. By the end of the day, your body might be done — but your mind keeps racing. In both environments, the early signs are easy to miss because they don't appear to be a failure. You're still showing up. You're still competent. You're still doing the job well. That's what makes it so deceptive. From the outside, nothing appears wrong. Inside, something essential is being slowly depleted. You might notice that days off no longer restore you. You wake up tired despite having slept. The thought of another shift brings a heaviness you can't quite explain. You start questioning things you never questioned before — not your skills, but your stamina. You wonder whether you've changed, whether you've lost something, or whether you're just not suited for this anymore.

That question — *"What's wrong with me?"* — is where burnout does the most damage.

Because it isn't a personal weakness, it's not a lack of resilience. It's not a failure to cope. Burnout occurs when a system repeatedly demands more than the human nervous system can reasonably provide, without sufficient recovery, control, or support in return. It's the body and mind signaling overload — not incompetence. Recognizing burnout isn't about giving up or labeling yourself as broken. It's about understanding what your experience is trying to tell you. When you can name burnout for what it is, you stop blaming yourself for a condition you didn't create. And that shift — from self-criticism to clarity — is where recovery begins.

This chapter isn't about telling you to "do less" or "be more resilient." It's about helping you understand how burnout actually forms in nursing environments, why it looks different in hospitals and ASCs, and how to reclaim your energy, confidence, and sense of purpose without losing the part of you that chose this profession in the first place. Burnout is not the end of your story.

It's the signal that something needs to change — and that change can begin with understanding.

BURNOUT IN NURSING
IS NOT ONE THING

One reason burnout feels so confusing in nursing is that it's often discussed as if it were a single condition with a single cause. It isn't. Burnout isn't a personality flaw or a failure to cope. It's a response — and that response looks different depending on the environment you work in.

Nursing is not one job. It's a profession practiced inside very different systems, each with its own pressures, expectations, and limits. When burnout is treated as a universal experience, nurses are left feeling misunderstood. A hospital nurse may receive advice that appears to have been written for someone working in a fast-paced, procedure-based setting. An ASC nurse may hear burnout described in ways that don't match the pace, precision, and constant urgency of her day. Both end up wondering if they're missing something — or if the problem is them. It does not. Burnout arises at the intersection of workload, emotional demand, control, and recovery. Change any one of those variables, and burnout changes shape. That's why two nurses can work just as hard, care just as deeply, and still burn out in entirely different ways.

In hospitals, it often builds slowly. It accumulates through

long shifts, repeated exposure to trauma, chronic understaffing, and the emotional weight of ongoing patient relationships. The work doesn't end when a task is completed. It
follows you through lab trends, evolving diagnoses, family
conversations, and unresolved outcomes. Hospital burnout
tends to feel heavy, draining, and persistent — like a slow
erosion of energy and identity.

In ASCs, it tends to be sharper and more immediate. The
pace is relentless. Turnovers are tight. Expectations are high.
There is little margin for error and even less time to recover
between cases. You may not carry patients' emotional
burdens for long periods, but you maintain intense focus,
precision, and responsibility for hours at a time. ASC burnout
often manifests as mental overload, irritability, and exhaustion that intensifies at the end of the day. Neither form is
"worse." They are simply different expressions of the same
underlying problem: the human nervous system being pushed
beyond sustainable limits.

What further complicates matters is that nurses are trained
to adapt. You adjust. You push through. You normalize strain
because caring has always required sacrifice. Over time, that
adaptability works against you. The body absorbs stress
quietly until one day it can no longer do so — and when that
happens, many nurses interpret the signal as personal weakness rather than systemic overload. That misunderstanding is
where burnout becomes dangerous.

When burnout isn't named correctly, nurses blame themselves. They assume they've lost resilience. They wonder
why they can't "handle it" like they used to. They compare
themselves to coworkers who seem fine and conclude they
must be failing in some invisible way. But burnout doesn't
mean you're failing nursing. It means nursing environments
are failing to support human limits. Understanding that

burnout is not one thing — and not one nurse's fault — is the first step toward recovery. Once you can identify *how* burnout forms in your specific environment, you stop fighting the wrong battle, you stop trying to fix yourself when what actually needs attention is the way your energy, attention, and care are being continuously extracted. From here, the work becomes clearer. Not easier — but clearer. And clarity is where power begins.

The Three Stages of Nurse Burnout

Burnout doesn't happen all at once. It unfolds in stages, often so gradually that nurses don't realize what's happening until they're already deep inside it. Understanding these stages matters because burnout feels overwhelming when it's unnamed — but it becomes manageable when you can recognize where you are and what's actually happening beneath the surface.

Most nurses don't wake up one day burned out. They slide there quietly, step by step, while still doing their jobs well.

Stage One — Overextension: "I can handle this."

Burnout often begins with competence. At this stage,
you're still functioning — sometimes exceptionally
well. You pick up extra shifts. You stay late when
needed. You absorb additional responsibilities
without complaint. You step in when staffing is tight,
when a coworker is overwhelmed, when the unit or
center needs someone dependable. In hospitals,
overextension often shows up as taking on more
patients, more emotional labor, more charting, and
more advocacy than the system realistically supports.
You compensate for shortages and inefficiencies
because patient care matters to you.

In ASCs, overextension looks like moving faster, tightening
turnovers, anticipating every need, managing personalities,
and maintaining precision without pause. You adjust your
own limits to keep the day running smoothly. At this stage,
burnout doesn't feel like burnout. It feels like professionalism. You tell yourself this is temporary once staffing
improves. Once schedules stabilize. Once things slow down.
You believe your capacity will catch up. What's actually
happening is quieter: your recovery is falling behind your
output.

Stage Two — Emotional Numbing: "I'm just tired."

When overextension continues without relief, the body
adapts. Not by producing more energy — but by conserving
it. This is the stage where many nurses notice subtle changes
in themselves. You're still doing the work, but with less
emotional engagement. You may experience detachment, irri-

tability, or flat affect. Tasks that once felt manageable now feel heavy. Conversations require more effort. You avoid unnecessary interaction, not out of hostility, but out of fatigue.

Hospital nurses may notice compassion fatigue emerging. You still care, but you don't feel it the same way. You may feel guilty about that detachment, which adds another layer of emotional strain. ASC nurses may experience increased irritability or impatience. The relentless pace leaves little room for emotional buffering, and the constant focus becomes exhausting rather than energizing. This stage is often misunderstood — especially by nurses themselves. Emotional numbing is not a lack of empathy. It's the nervous system protecting itself from overload. When caring becomes too costly, the system reduces the volume. Many nurses get stuck here because the work continues to be done. There's no obvious crisis. But the cost is growing.

Stage Three — Disengagement: "I don't know if I can do this anymore."

When emotional numbing persists, burnout moves into disengagement. This is the stage at which burnout becomes impossible to ignore. Disengagement doesn't always look dramatic. Sometimes it looks like silence. You stop speaking up. You stop offering ideas. You do exactly what's required — no more, no less. You begin emotionally checking out before your shift even starts. In hospitals, this stage is often accompanied by a desire to leave the unit, change roles, or exit bedside nursing altogether. You may feel disconnected from your professional identity, unsure whether you're still the nurse you once were. In ASCs, disengagement can feel like constant frustration or resentment. The pace that once energized you now feels suffocating. You may fantasize about slower work, fewer cases, or a different environment entirely. This stage is frightening because it challenges identity. Nurses often interpret disengagement as failure — proof that they're no longer cut out for the profession. In reality, disengagement is not a character flaw. It's a signal that endurance has reached its limit.

Why These Stages Matter

Recognizing these stages changes how you relate to burnout. Instead of asking, *"What's wrong with me?"* you begin asking, *"Where am I in this process?"*

Burnout is not a sudden collapse. It's unaddressed overextension followed by self-protection and, eventually, withdrawal. The earlier you recognize the pattern, the more options you have. Recovery is far easier in the overextension stage than in complete disengagement — but recovery is possible at every stage once burnout is named without shame. Understanding the stages also removes moral judgment. You didn't become burned out because you stopped caring. You continued to care long after the system had ceased to support it. Burnout is not a personal failure. It's a predictable response to sustained imbalance. Recognizing which stage you're in is not discouraging — it's empowering. Because understanding is the first step toward change, and change is what turns burnout from an ending into a turning point.

WHY BURNOUT FEELS PERSONAL (EVEN WHEN IT ISN'T)

One of the most painful parts of burnout is not the exhaustion itself — it's the way it quietly turns into self-blame. Long before nurses say "I'm burned out," many start asking themselves a much harsher question: *What's wrong with me?*

Burnout feels personal because nursing is personal. You don't show up to this work by accident. You bring a sense of responsibility, pride, and care that extends far beyond a job description. Your identity is tied to competence, dependability, and emotional presence. When something starts to feel off — when your patience shortens, your focus slips, or your motivation fades — it strikes at who you believe you are, not just what you do.

Nursing culture reinforces this internalization. From the beginning, nurses are praised for endurance. Pushing through is framed as professionalism. Sacrifice is normalized. When you succeed under pressure, it's seen as proof of strength. When you struggle, it's often framed — implicitly or explicitly — as a lack of resilience. Over time, that messaging teaches nurses to interpret exhaustion as a personal failure rather than a predictable response to sustained overload.

Burnout also feels personal because it doesn't arrive with
clear external markers. You're still showing up. You're still
performing. Your patients may be safe. Your coworkers may
not notice anything different. From the outside, you look fine.
Inside, you feel depleted. That disconnect makes it easy to
assume the problem must be internal—that something within
you has changed or weakened.

For hospital nurses, this personalizing often shows up as
guilt. You may feel guilty for not having the same emotional
bandwidth you once did, for dreading another shift, or for
feeling detached when you believe you *should* feel compassion. You may question your commitment or wonder if you're
losing the part of you that made you a good nurse in the first
place. For ASC nurses, burnout often masquerades as irritability or impatience. You may feel frustrated by inefficiency, become short-tempered under pressure, or resent
constant urgency. Because the environment values speed and
precision, emotional exhaustion is easily misinterpreted as an
attitude problem rather than a capacity problem.

In both settings, burnout distorts perspective. It narrows
your view until every struggle feels like a personal shortcoming. You begin measuring yourself against who you used to
be rather than against what your current environment requires
of you. That comparison is almost always unfair.

What's actually happening is simpler — and kinder —
than the story burnout tells. Your nervous system is over-
loaded. Your emotional reserves are depleted. Your capacity
has been exceeded for too long without adequate recovery or
control. None of that says anything about your skill, your
dedication, or your worth. Burnout feels personal because it
attacks the parts of you that care the most. It doesn't target
indifference. It targets commitment. Because nurses care

deeply, they are especially vulnerable to interpreting burnout as a personal flaw rather than as an environmental signal.

Understanding this distinction is critical. The moment you separate *who you are* from *what you're experiencing*, the shame begins to loosen its grip. You stop asking, "Why can't I handle this?" and start asking, "What has this environment been requiring of me?" That shift doesn't excuse poor systems — but it does protect your sense of self. Burnout is not evidence that you're failing nursing. It's evidence that nursing has been asked to do more than is sustainable. When you can see burnout clearly — not as a verdict on your character but as information about your circumstances — you create space for recovery. And that clarity becomes the foundation for the changes that follow.

PSYCHOLOGICAL
SAFETY AND BURNOUT

Burnout doesn't come only from long hours or heavy workloads. It accelerates when you don't feel safe — emotionally, professionally, or psychologically — in the environment where you work. Psychological safety is the invisible factor that determines whether stress drains you temporarily or depletes you permanently. Psychological safety means being able to speak up, ask questions, clarify, or express concerns without fear of embarrassment, punishment, or retaliation. It means knowing that raising a hand won't cost you credibility, your reputation, or your job. When that safety is missing, the nervous system stays on guard, even during moments that should be routine. A guarded nervous system degrades quickly.

In hospital settings, the absence of psychological safety often hides behind systems and policy. Nurses may hesitate to speak up because they've seen what happens when someone does. Concerns get redirected into documentation, audits, or "education." Patterns get labeled as isolated incidents. Feedback becomes impersonal, filtered, or delayed. Over time, nurses learn that it's safer to stay quiet than to risk being misunderstood or flagged. The work continues, but the voice disappears. In ASCs, psychological safety is shaped more by proximity than policy. Small teams, strong personalities, and tightly packed schedules create environments where reactions are immediate and visible. A raised eyebrow, a sharp comment, or a dismissive tone can linger for the rest of the day. When nurses sense that speaking up will lead to tension, retaliation, or subtle exclusion, they adapt by becoming quieter, faster, and more cautious. That constant self-monitoring drains energy in ways few people recognize.

In both environments, the result is the same: nurses stop bringing their complete awareness to the room. Not because they don't care, but because caring out loud feels risky. They choose silence over advocacy, compliance over clarity, and emotional withdrawal over engagement. Each of those choices may protect them in the moment — but over time, they hollow out confidence and purpose. Psychological safety matters because nursing requires judgment. It requires noticing patterns, questioning assumptions, and responding to subtle changes. When nurses don't feel safe to trust their own perceptions, they second-guess themselves. They hesitate. They delay. That internal friction is exhausting. It turns every decision into a calculation: *Is this worth speaking up about? Is this going to come back on me?*

Burnout thrives in that uncertainty.

What's especially damaging is that nurses often internalize the lack of safety as a personal issue. They tell themselves they're "too sensitive" or "not assertive enough." They assume they need to toughen up or adapt better. In reality, no amount of resilience can compensate for an environment that punishes clarity and discourages voice. When psychological safety is present, stress still exists — but it doesn't accumulate in the same way. Nurses can speak, correct, clarify, and decompress in real time. Tension moves through the system instead of lodging in the body. Mistakes become learning moments rather than identity threats. Work remains demanding, but it doesn't erode the sense of self. This is why burnout recovery isn't only about rest. It's about restoring the ability to show up fully without fear. Whether you work in a hospital or an ASC, psychological safety determines whether your energy is spent on patient care — or on protecting yourself.

Recognizing the role of psychological safety reframes burnout from a personal struggle to an environmental signal. It helps you see why exhaustion deepens in places where silence feels safer than honesty. And it sets the stage for the next shift: learning how to protect your confidence, your voice, and your well-being even when the environment itself hasn't caught up yet.

HOSPITAL BURNOUT:
THE SLOW EROSION

Hospital burnout rarely feels sudden. It doesn't arrive as a breaking point or a dramatic collapse. Instead, it works quietly, wearing you down over time in ways that are easy to rationalize and hard to name. That's what makes it so powerful — and so damaging. In a hospital, the demands don't come in neat, contained bursts. They span shifts, weeks, and patient stays that don't end well. You don't just complete tasks; you carry responsibility forward. You track trends. You anticipate decline. You hold concern long before anything officially "goes wrong." That ongoing vigilance keeps patients safe, but it also keeps your nervous system engaged long after your shift ends.

Hospital nurses live inside continuity. You care for patients through uncertainty, setbacks, and slow progress. You watch families oscillate between hope and fear. You absorb grief, frustration, and anger — often without space to process any of it. There's rarely time to pause and acknowledge what you've witnessed before the next call light goes off or the next admission arrives. Over time, that emotional exposure accumulates. It doesn't always feel dramatic. Sometimes it just feels heavy. You start the day already tired. You feel a dull sense of pressure in your chest or shoulders that never fully releases. You notice that your empathy is still there, but accessing it takes more effort than it used to. That's not a failure of compassion — it's a sign of depletion.

Staffing plays a central role in this erosion. Chronic short staffing forces you into impossible choices: which patient needs you most right now, which task can wait, and where corners might be unintentionally cut. You know what safe, thorough care looks like. You also know that time, resources, and staffing often don't allow for it. Living inside that gap — between what should be done and what can be done — creates moral distress that slowly drains your sense of professional integrity. Documentation adds another layer. Charting is meant to protect patients and nurses, but when documentation demands multiply without regard for time or staffing, it becomes another source of pressure. You carry the weight of knowing that how something is written may matter as much as — or more than — how it was handled clinically. That constant awareness keeps part of your mind braced, even during moments that should be routine.

Hospital burnout is also shaped by invisibility. In large systems, excellent work often goes unnoticed. You stabilize a patient, prevent a complication, de-escalate a crisis — and then move on without acknowledgment. Over time, that lack of recognition can make even the most competent nurse feel unseen. Not unskilled. Unseen. What makes hospital burnout especially difficult is that it often coexists with deep commitment. You still care. You still advocate. You still attend to your patients. From the outside, you look fine. From the inside, you may feel flattened — less curious, less engaged, less like yourself. That internal change can be frightening, especially for nurses who identify strongly with their compassion and professionalism.

As hospital burnout progresses, many nurses notice subtle shifts in behavior. You may stop volunteering for extras. You may avoid difficult conversations simply because you don't have the energy. You may go quiet in meetings where you once spoke up. These aren't signs of disengagement — they are signs of self-preservation. Eventually, the exhaustion becomes harder to ignore. Days off don't restore you the way they used to. Sleep doesn't feel refreshing. The idea of another stretch of shifts feels overwhelming, even if nothing specific is "wrong." That's the slow erosion at work — not dramatic, not sudden, but deeply impactful.

Hospital burnout doesn't mean you're not strong enough for the job. It means you've been strong for too long without enough recovery, control, or support. It's the predictable result of sustained emotional labor, responsibility without relief, and systems that rely on nurses' adaptability to absorb chronic strain—understanding it as erosion, not failure, matters. When you can see it clearly, you stop questioning your worth or your resilience. You begin to recognize that what you're feeling is a signal, not a verdict. That recognition creates an opening for change.

ASC BURNOUT: THE
RELENTLESS PACE

Burnout in an ASC doesn't usually build slowly. It arrives through speed, repetition, and intensity — day after day — until your nervous system never quite powers down. Unlike hospital burnout, which erodes over time, ASC burnout often feels sharp, immediate, and surprisingly physical. In an ASC, the workday is defined by momentum. Cases stack. Turnovers compress. Schedules leave little margin for delay. From the moment the first patient arrives, the expectation is clear: move efficiently, stay precise, don't miss anything, and keep everything flowing. There is no natural pause between demands. The next patient is always ready, the next case already planned, the clock already ticking. That constant forward motion requires sustained focus. You're not just performing tasks — you're maintaining rhythm. You antici-pate needs before they're voiced. You manage equipment, timing, safety, documentation, and personalities all at once. Precision matters, speed matters, and mistakes are highly visible. That level of cognitive load, sustained for hours at a time, depletes energy more quickly than most people realize.

ASC burnout is also shaped by visibility. In small teams,

everything is noticed. When something goes well, it's expected. When something doesn't, it's immediately apparent. There's little anonymity and even less room to blend into the background. You're "on" from start to finish — observed, evaluated, and often silently judged by people who may not understand the full scope of what you're managing. Surgeon-driven urgency adds another layer. In many ASCs, surgeons carry significant influence over the day's tone, pace, and priorities. Their schedules, preferences, and moods can shape the entire environment. Even when interactions are professional, the underlying pressure to keep cases moving creates a constant sense of urgency. Nurses often absorb that pressure quietly, adjusting their own pace and expectations to keep the day running smoothly.

What makes ASC burnout particularly exhausting is the combination of intensity and repetition. The cases may be shorter, but the mental demand doesn't reset between them. There's rarely time to process what just happened before you're preparing for what's next. Over time, that lack of recovery accumulates. You may finish the day feeling mentally fried, irritable, or strangely detached — even though nothing "went wrong." ASC nurses often struggle to name their burnout because the environment can look efficient and controlled from the outside. There's no long-term patient decline. No extended trauma exposure. No unresolved outcomes carried over weeks. And yet, the exhaustion is real. It manifests as tension, headaches, jaw clenching, shallow breathing, or a racing mind that won't quiet down after work. Another hidden contributor is emotional labor. Even in highly professional centers, nurses frequently manage the emotional climate of the room — smoothing tension, anticipating reactions, adjusting communication styles, and preventing friction before it escalates. That work is invisible, unacknowledged, and draining. It requires emotional awareness layered on top of technical precision, and it's rarely counted when people assess workload.

As burnout deepens, nurses may notice subtle shifts. You become less patient with minor disruptions. You feel irritated by inefficiency, even when it isn't your fault. You stop engaging beyond what's required, not because you don't care, but because you don't have anything left to give. You may start fantasizing about slower work, different roles, or leaving altogether — even if you once loved the pace. It doesn't mean you can't handle fast environments. It means the pace has been relentless, with insufficient recovery, autonomy, or acknowledgment. It's what happens when efficiency becomes the primary value and human limits are treated as inconveniences rather than realities.

Understanding burnout as a response to sustained intensity — not a lack of resilience — changes how you relate to it. You stop blaming yourself for feeling worn down by a system designed to run at full speed all day, every day. And once you recognize that, you're in a position to make adjustments that restore your energy without abandoning your skills or your professionalism.

BURNOUT BEHAVIORS: HOSPITAL VS ASC

Although burnout behaviors follow similar patterns, they tend to express themselves differently depending on where you work. Understanding these differences helps you recognize burnout sooner — and respond more accurately.

In **hospital settings**, burnout behaviors often develop quietly and inwardly. Nurses may become more emotionally reserved over time, especially after repeated exposure to trauma, grief, or moral distress. You might notice yourself pulling back emotionally, limiting conversations to what's strictly necessary, or feeling numb during situations that once moved you. Advocacy may decline, not because you've stopped noticing problems, but because you've learned that raising concerns often leads to documentation, scrutiny, or delayed response rather than resolution.

Hospital burnout also shows up as mental fatigue. You may feel overwhelmed by charting, policies, audits, or competing directives. Decision-making feels heavier. The constant need to remember protocols, documentation require-ments, and escalation pathways keeps part of your mind constantly on alert. Over time, this can create a sense of invisibility — the feeling that no matter how much you do, it disappears into the system.

In **ASC'S**, burnout behaviors tend to be sharper and more outwardly noticeable. The pace leaves little room to disengage quietly, so it often surfaces as irritability, impatience, or rigidity. You may find yourself becoming highly task-focused, intolerant of inefficiency, or frustrated by anything that disrupts flow. Because teams are small and interactions are constant, emotional exhaustion may show up as shorter responses, reduced tolerance for personality clashes, or a strong desire to "just get through the day." ASC nurses may also notice increased hyper-vigilance. You stay tightly focused, anticipate needs, prevent errors, and manage timing without pause. While this appears to be competence, it often feels like constant tension. There's little opportunity to reset between cases mentally, and the lack of recovery time compounds exhaustion quickly.

In both environments, these behaviors are frequently misunderstood by others and by the nurses themselves. Hospital nurses may assume their emotional withdrawal means they've lost compassion. ASC nurses may assume their impatience means they're no longer suited for fast-paced work. In reality, both are adaptive responses to prolonged pressure. Burnout doesn't change your values. It changes how your nervous system protects you. Recognizing how burnout manifests in your specific environment helps you respond with clarity rather than self-criticism.

BURNOUT BEHAVIORS:
HOSPITAL VS ASC

Burnout Behaviors Self-Check

This self-check isn't a diagnosis. It's a moment of awareness. You don't need to fix anything right now — just notice.

Read each statement and ask yourself whether it feels familiar lately.

You may be experiencing burnout-related behaviors if:

- You speak less at work than you used to, even when you have something valuable to say
- You avoid unnecessary conversations because they feel draining
- You feel irritated by small inefficiencies or interruptions
- You stop advocating unless the issue feels critical
- You over-explain, over-apologize, or carefully manage how others feel
- You feel emotionally flat or detached, even though you still care

- You focus on tasks because engaging emotionally feels like too much
- You feel more tense at work, and it doesn't fully release when you go home
- You tell yourself you "just need to push through" more often than before
- You miss feeling like yourself at work

If several of these resonate, it doesn't mean you're failing. It means your system has been working hard to protect you.

The purpose of this self-check is not to create alarm — it's to create honesty. Burnout becomes more difficult to recover from when it remains unnamed. When you recognize these behaviors early, you give yourself options. You regain the ability to choose how to respond, rather than endure. Awareness is where control begins.

WHY REST OR VACATION
ALONE DOESN'T FIX BURNOUT

Rest is necessary. But rest alone is not enough.

Many nurses reach burnout and assume the solution is time off — a few days away, a vacation, a lighter schedule. While rest can offer temporary relief, it often fails to produce lasting change. Nurses return to work hoping they'll feel different, only to realize that the heaviness comes back almost immediately. That experience can be discouraging and often leads to a painful conclusion: *if rest didn't help, something must be wrong with me.* Nothing could be further from the truth.

Rest restores energy, but burnout is not only an energy problem. It is also a control problem, a meaning problem, and a safety problem. When those factors remain unchanged, rest becomes a short pause in an ongoing drain rather than a proper reset. In nursing environments, much of the exhaustion comes from sustained vigilance. You're not just physically active — you're constantly assessing, anticipating, and adjusting. The nervous system stays activated for hours at a time. When you step away, that activation may decrease briefly, but if you return to the same demands, the system quickly re-enters high-alert mode. The cycle repeats. A vacation is meaningless if you return to the same issues.

Rest also doesn't resolve moral distress. Hospital nurses may return to the same problems, the same documentation pressure, the same ethical discomfort of knowing what care *should* look like and being unable to deliver it consistently. ASC nurses may return to the same relentless pace, the same urgency, the same expectation of perfection without recovery time. No amount of sleep can resolve the stress of repeated value conflicts. Another reason that resting alone falls short is that burnout often entails emotional and cognitive depletion. When you've spent months or years managing emotions — your own and everyone else's — taking time off doesn't automatically rebuild that capacity. Emotional reserves are restored by safety, autonomy, and meaningful control, not merely by their absence.

There's also the reality that many nurses don't truly rest when they're off. The mind stays busy. The body stays tense. You may spend days off catching up on life, managing responsibilities, or mentally preparing to return. Without a sense of purpose or change, time off becomes maintenance rather than recovery. You can run, but you can't hide. Recovery requires something rest can't provide on its own: a change in how your energy is being spent. It requires reducing unnecessary strain, reclaiming small areas of control, and redefining expectations — both external and internal. This doesn't mean quitting or dramatically altering your career overnight. It means recognizing that returning to the same environment with the same patterns will produce the same exhaustion. Proper recovery begins when rest is paired with intention.

When rest is combined with understanding, something shifts. You stop using time off to merely survive the next stretch and start using it to support a different way of working. You identify what drains you the most. You decide what you will no longer carry alone. You begin making changes — even small ones — that alter the equation. Rest is the foundation, not the solution. Burnout eases when rest is paired with control, safety, and meaningful choice. Without those elements, time off becomes a temporary bandage. With them, rest becomes restorative again.

Understanding this is not discouraging — it's empowering. It explains why burnout didn't resolve with a weekend away and points you toward what actually will help. And that understanding prepares you for the most important shift of all: the recovery pivot.

BURNOUT AND PERSONAL RELATIONSHIPS: ASC NURSE VS. HOSPITAL NURSE

ASC Nurse Example

Karen works as an ASC nurse. On paper, her job looks manageable—predictable hours, no overnights, no codes. But the pace is relentless. Cases are stacked back-to-back. Turnover time is scrutinized. Efficiency is everything. At work, Karen is "on" constantly. She reassures anxious patients, keeps surgeons on schedule, manages anesthesia coordination, and handles families who expect flawless outcomes. Errors are not tolerated, and delays are quietly attributed to nursing. By the time she gets home, she is not physically exhausted—she is **mentally stripped down**.

When her partner wants to talk, Karen feels pressured rather than connected. Questions like "How was your day?" feel loaded. Decision-making feels unbearable. Even low-stakes choices—dinner plans, weekend errands—trigger irritation. She begins withdrawing emotionally. Not dramatically. Just less engagement. Shorter answers. Less enthusiasm. Less patience.

Her partner notices:

- She seems "checked out."
- She avoids conversations
- She wants silence instead of closeness.

Karen doesn't feel depressed. She feels **used up**. All of her attentiveness and emotional control have already been spent at work. Over time, the relationship starts to feel like another performance she no longer has the energy to maintain.

Hospital Nurse Example

Monica works on a hospital unit. Staffing shortages mean she regularly cares for more patients than is reasonable. She forms attachments—patients she sees day after day, families she gets to know, outcomes she cannot control. She absorbs anger, fear, grief, and blame during every shift. She holds it together professionally, even when situations deteriorate or become emotionally charged. At home, the emotional fallout appears differently.

She becomes hyper-irritable over small things. She is easily overwhelmed by noise, questions, or requests. She either talks too little or unloads everything at once—neither of which feels satisfying to her partner. Physical affection feels intrusive instead of comforting. Intimacy requires vulnerability, and Monica has spent all day protecting herself emotionally. Her partner feels pushed away. Monica feels misunderstood and resentful—because she is already giving more than she has. The relationship slowly shifts from partnership to coexistence.

THE KEY DIFFERENCE

- **ASC burnout** often looks like *emotional flatness and withdrawal*
- **Hospital burnout** often looks like *irritability, overload, and emotional spillover*

In both cases, the common thread is this: Burnout narrows emotional capacity. Relationships suffer not from lack of love, but from lack of remaining bandwidth.

CHRONIC EMOTIONAL OVER-RESPONSIBILITY

Many nurses—particularly women—carry a form of responsibility that extends far beyond clinical duties. They are accountable not only for tasks and outcomes but also for the emotional climate surrounding care. Over time, this responsibility becomes internalized and automatic. A nurse does not simply provide care. She monitors tone. She anticipates reactions. She absorbs tension. She adjusts herself to maintain calm, cooperation, and reassurance—often without realizing she is doing it. In both ASCs and hospitals, patient satisfaction has become a de facto metric. Nurses feel personally accountable for how patients and families feel, even when fear, pain, unrealistic expectations, or systemic delays shape those feelings. When a patient is anxious or dissatisfied, the nurse often attributes this to a personal shortcoming rather than to situational factors.

Family emotions add another layer. Nurses routinely absorb frustration, grief, anger, and fear, acting as emotional buffers between the patient's family and the system. They de-escalate, reassure, and explain—often taking on emotional weight that does not belong to them. When families are upset, the nurse may carry a sense of responsibility long after the interaction ends.

==========

A Common Scenario

A patient's family member is upset because:

- A procedure is delayed
- They don't understand what's happening
- They're scared of an outcome
- They feel ignored, dismissed, or powerless

Even when the cause is unrelated to nursing—staffing, scheduling, physician availability, insurance, or policy—the family directs their fear and frustration toward the nurse because she is present and accessible.

The nurse responds professionally:

- She lowers her tone
- She listens without correcting
- She explains the situation carefully
- She reassures, even when certainty isn't possible

In that moment, she is not just providing information. She is regulating the room's emotional temperature.

==========

Conflict within the healthcare system further reinforces this pattern. Nurses frequently mediate tension among providers, departments, and administrative policies. When systems fail or communication breaks down, nurses become the human interface. They apologize for delays they did not create and justify decisions they did not make. This creates a subtle yet powerful internal message: *if something feels wrong, it must be my responsibility to fix.* Even when situations are clearly outside the nurse's control, the emotional residue lingers. She replays conversations. She wonders what she could have said differently. She carries concern home— not because she is ineffective, but because she has been conditioned to hold responsibility that exceeds her authority. Over time, this chronic emotional over-responsibility reshapes the inner landscape.

The nurse experiences persistent guilt, even on days when she performed well. She engages in self-blame for outcomes she could not influence. She struggles to mentally "put the day down," because emotionally unresolved moments continue to demand attention. This pattern does not come from weakness. It comes from empathy, conscientiousness, and a deep sense of duty—qualities that are praised in nursing, but rarely protected. Without intentional boundaries, emotional over-responsibility becomes a quiet form of self-erasure. The nurse remains capable and committed, yet increasingly burdened by feelings that were never hers to carry.

CHRONIC EMOTIONAL OVER-RESPONSIBILITY (ASC VS. HOSPITAL)

How It Shows Up in ASCs

In ASCs, emotional over-responsibility is closely tied to efficiency, satisfaction, and control. ASC nurses often feel personally responsible for keeping the day running smoothly—not only clinically but also emotionally. When schedules run behind, when patients are anxious, or when surgeons are frustrated, the nurse becomes the emotional shock absorber. Because ASCs emphasize speed, predictability, and patient satisfaction, nurses may internalize the belief that *any disruption is a personal failure.*

Common ASC-specific patterns include:

- Feeling responsible when a patient is anxious, upset, or dissatisfied—even if the cause is outside nursing control

- Absorbing pressure from surgeons or anesthesia to "keep things moving."
- Apologizing for delays caused by scheduling, equipment, or administrative decisions
- Monitoring everyone's mood to prevent tension or conflict

ASC nurses often leave work replaying interactions, wondering how they could have kept things smoother, calmer, or more pleasant—despite having done their job well. Emotionally, the message becomes:

If the environment isn't calm, I didn't manage it well enough.

How It Shows Up in Hospitals

In hospital settings, emotional over-responsibility is driven more by complexity, acuity, and continuity. Hospital nurses often develop deeper emotional ties to patients and families because care unfolds over days or weeks. As a result, nurses may feel personally accountable not only for care but also for outcomes, emotional reactions, and family coping.

Common hospital-specific patterns include:

- Feeling responsible for family distress, even when outcomes are poor or unpredictable
- Carrying guilt over patient declines, complications, or difficult conversations

- Acting as a mediator between families, providers, and systems
- Feeling pressure to absorb anger or fear without expressing frustration

Because hospitals involve ongoing relationships, nurses may carry emotional weight long after shifts end—thinking about patients at home, worrying on days off, and feeling responsible even when they are not present. Emotionally, the message becomes: *If someone is suffering, I should be able to help more.*

THE EMOTIONAL COST

IN BOTH ENVIRONMENTS, THE NURSE BECOMES RESPONSIBLE FOR FAR MORE THAN SHE CAN REASONABLY CONTROL. OVER TIME, THIS CREATES:

- Persistent guilt
- Self-blame for systemic problems
- Difficulty mentally disengaging after work
- Emotional fatigue that does not resolve with rest

The nurse does not just leave work tired—she leaves work **emotionally entangled**.

SELF-RECOGNITION CHECKLIST

Signs of Chronic Emotional Over-Responsibility

You may be carrying emotional responsibility that does not belong to you if you:

- Replay conversations from work long after your shift ends
- Feel guilty when patients or families are upset, even when you followed protocol
- Apologize for delays or decisions you did not create
- Feel responsible for keeping everyone calm or satisfied
- Take on the role of mediator or peacekeeper automatically
- Struggle to emotionally "put the day down" once you're home
- Feel uneasy or restless on days off, thinking about work situations
- Assume that conflict or dissatisfaction reflects a personal failure
- Feel emotionally drained without a clear reason why
- Rarely ask yourself, *"Is this actually mine to carry?"*

If several of these resonate, it does not mean you are doing something wrong. It means you are doing **too much emotionally**, often without realizing it. Emotional over-responsibility frequently develops from strength—empathy, reliability, and professionalism. But when responsibility extends beyond control, it becomes unsustainable. Learning to distinguish **what is yours to hold** from **what is yours to witness** is not detachment. It is preservation.

4

THE RECOVERY PIVOT:
WHAT ACTUALLY HELPS

B urnout recovery doesn't begin with a vacation, a
schedule change, or a promise to "take better care of
yourself." Those things can help, but they don't
address the core issue. Burnout recovers when you stop
asking, *"How do I survive this?"* and start asking, *"What is
draining me — and what control do I actually have?"* The
pivot happens when you realize that burnout is not a
command to leave nursing or abandon who you are. It's an
invitation to change how you use your energy. Most nurses
don't burn out because they care too much. They burn out
because their care, attention, and emotional labor are spread
everywhere without boundaries, recovery, or choice.

Recovery starts when you recognize what is within your
control and act on it. That doesn't mean fixing the system
overnight. It means identifying where you are wasting energy
and deliberately deciding where you will no longer spend it.
For some nurses, this is the first time they have paused long
enough to notice how much effort goes into tasks that are not
actually part of patient care: managing moods, anticipating
reactions, smoothing over dysfunction, remaining silent to

avoid conflict, or carrying responsibility that was never truly theirs. When you begin to see those patterns clearly, something significant changes. You stop interpreting exhaustion as a personal failure and start treating it as information. You ask better questions. *What part of my day drains me the fastest? What conversations leave me depleted? Where am I giving more than I'm required to give?* Those answers become your starting point.

Recovery also involves restoring a sense of control during the shift itself. Burnout thrives in environments where everything feels reactive. Even small pockets of predictability and choice can calm the nervous system. That might look like organizing your workflow to reduce decision fatigue, preparing steady phrases for complicated interactions, or permitting yourself to step back emotionally when a situation isn't yours to carry. This is not disengagement. It's discernment. Another critical part of the pivot is separating your worth from your output. Nursing culture often rewards endurance — the nurse who stays late, picks up extra, never complains, and absorbs pressure quietly. Over time, that identity becomes dangerous. Recovery requires redefining what it means to be a "good nurse." Competence does not require exhaustion. Commitment does not require self-erasure. Professionalism does not require suffering.

For hospital nurses, the recovery pivot often involves assessing whether the current unit, schedule, or role continues to support their capacity. Sometimes recovery means lateral movement, not exit — a different unit, a different shift pattern, or a role that uses your skills without constant emotional depletion. For ASC nurses, the pivot may involve renegotiating pace expectations, clarifying roles, or choosing culture over convenience when deciding where to work. What recovery does *not* require is becoming less caring or less invested. It requires becoming more intentional.

The final component of the recovery pivot is permission —permission to change without waiting until you're completely depleted. Many nurses believe they must reach a breaking point before they're allowed to adjust course. In reality, the earlier you respond to burnout signals, the faster and more fully you recover. Recovery isn't about becoming a different nurse. It's about returning to yourself with more clarity and less sacrifice. Once you understand what drains you and what restores you, burnout loses its power to define your future. It becomes a chapter — not the whole story. From that place, you can begin rebuilding your work life in a way that supports not only your patients but also you.

RECOVERY PIVOT: A STEP-BY-STEP GUIDE YOU CAN USE

Step 1: Name what you're experiencing—accurately

Instead of "I'm failing" or "I'm just tired," call it what it is:

- "I'm depleted."
- "I'm burning out."
- "My workload and stress have exceeded my recovery."

This reduces shame and gives you a problem you can solve.

Step 2: Identify your burnout type

Ask: *What is most draining?*

- **Hospital:** emotional load, moral distress, staffing ratios, bureaucracy, documentation

- **ASC:** pace pressure, turnover demand, high visibility, surgeon-driven urgency, constant hyper-focus

You can't fix what you can't define.

Step 3: Find your "fastest drain"

Pick the one factor that wipes you out the quickest:

- a specific interaction pattern (being snapped at, dismissed, blamed)
- a recurring workflow issue (constant add-ons, unclear handoffs)
- a physical issue (no breaks, no hydration, constant running)
- a system issue (charting after shift, impossible ratios)

Choose **one** drain to target first. Burnout improves fastest when you stop trying to fix everything at once.

Step 4: Reduce invisible emotional labor

Ask yourself: *Where am I managing feelings that aren't mine to manage?*

Examples:

- Smoothing over conflict so the team stays calm
- Overexplaining to avoid someone's reaction
- Taking responsibility for other people's urgency
- Apologizing to keep the peace

Your pivot starts when you stop spending energy on emotional work that isn't required.

Step 5: Build a "steady script" for blame, pressure, or dismissal

Pick 2–3 phrases you will use consistently so you don't have to invent language when you're stressed:

- "Here's what happened on my end."
- "For clarity, my understanding is…"
- "Let's confirm the plan, so we're aligned."
- "I can do X now, and Y next. Which is the priority?"

This is a major pivot tool because it turns chaos into structure.

Step 6: Reclaim micro-control during your shift

Even in a broken system, you can create small pockets of control that calm your nervous system.

Examples:

- Start-of-shift 2-minute plan (top priorities, likely problems)
- A consistent workflow "reset" between patients/cases
- One protected break ritual (water, breathing, quick walk)
- A hard stop on unnecessary extras ("I can't take that on today.")

Burnout worsens when everything feels reactive. Micro-control restores stability.

Step 7: Document what protects you—not what punishes you

Documentation isn't about building a case. It's about preventing reality from being rewritten later.

Use neutral language:

- "Per discussion at 10:15, plan is ___."
- "Delay related to ___; action taken ___."

Hospital nurses should prioritize documentation that protects accuracy and context.

ASC nurses should focus on clarity around orders, timing, and workflow.

Step 8: Make one structural change within 14 days

Recovery requires at least one *real* change, even if small:

- Adjust availability or overtime habits
- Stop picking up an extra role you resent
- Request consistent scheduling
- transfer units (hospital)
- shift to a different center/culture (ASC)
- change your role mix (pre-op/PACU/OR balance)

No change = no pivot. Even a small one counts.

Step 9: Build a support point outside the shift

Choose one:

- a trusted coworker you can reality-check with
- a mentor/educator/charge nurse you respect
- a professional group where nurses discuss issues (not gossip)
- therapy/coaching if burnout is deep or prolonged

Burnout isolates. Recovery reconnects.

Step 10: Decide your "line in the sand"

This is the most empowering step.

Ask yourself:

- "What will I no longer tolerate?"
- "What will I do if this continues?"

Examples:

- If staffing stays unsafe → request transfer or reduced hours
- If surgeon behavior stays volatile → escalate through proper channels/change centers
- If documentation pressure is punitive → seek a different unit, role, or environment

A pivot isn't just coping better. It's choosing a future where your limits are respected.

Step 11: Run a 2-week check

After two weeks, ask:

- "What improved?"
- "What didn't?"
- "What is my next smallest change?"

Recovery unfolds over time, shaped by the decisions you make along the way.

5

QUIET EXIT FANTASIES: BURNOUT'S FINAL PSYCHOLOGICAL SIGNAL

Burnout rarely begins with a desire to leave the profession. For most nurses, the thought of leaving arrives much later—after endurance, adaptation, and self-sacrifice have already been exhausted. What appears first is something quieter.

A nurse does not say, *"I want to quit."*

She thinks, *"I can't keep doing this forever."*

This distinction matters. Quiet exit fantasies are not impulsive or dramatic. They are mental pressure valves—brief imaginings of relief when the nervous system can no longer fully recover between shifts. They surface when burnout has progressed from fatigue into **chronic depletion**.

How Burnout Produces Exit Fantasies

Burnout gradually compresses a nurse's internal world until survival tasks dominate it. The workday is no longer organized around purpose, learning, or professional growth. It becomes organized around endurance. You wake up focused on one objective: getting through the shift. Not excelling, not connecting. Not improving, just getting through.

During the shift, attention narrows further. Every ounce of cognitive and emotional energy is directed toward keeping patients safe and avoiding mistakes. The stakes are constant and unforgiving. Errors are not abstract—they can alter lives, careers, or both. This sustained vigilance leaves no space for reflection or forward thinking. There is only the immediate present and the next problem to solve. By the end of the day, the final goal is simple: make it home. Not restored. Not fulfilled. Just intact.

When this pattern repeats day after day, your sense of time changes; the future no longer feels expandable. There is no room in the role to imagine growth, evolution, or meaning. The job no longer contains a viable long-term path—only an endless series of shifts to survive. When human beings cannot locate a future inside their current structure, the mind does what it is designed to do: it searches for an exit. This search does not reflect a lack of commitment or compassion. It reflects a system that has consumed all available capacity without allowing renewal.

Exit fantasies emerge quietly. They often appear as fleeting daydreams rather than conscious decisions. You imagine doing something "simpler"—not because the work itself is beneath her skill, but because simplicity represents psychological relief. She imagines a job where mistakes are inconvenient rather than catastrophic. A role where responsibility ends when the shift ends. Sometimes the fantasy is not about another job at all, but about anonymity. Being one of many, unneeded, and unobserved. Not having to carry outcomes, emotions, or lives on her shoulders. These thoughts are not escape plans. They are diagnostic signals. They indicate that the nervous system has been operating in sustained threat mode. They signal that the current structure no longer offers a sense of the future; it only repeats. They are the mind's attempt to restore balance by imagining conditions where recovery might be possible. Ignoring these signals does not make them disappear. It forces you to remain in a narrowed internal world—functional, responsible, and increasingly depleted—until something eventually gives. Burnout is not the absence of resilience. It is the consequence of resilience being used without recovery.

Why Nurses Don't Talk About Them

Quiet exit fantasies are often accompanied by guilt. Nursing is framed as a calling. Many nurses invested years of education, identity, and sacrifice into the role. Admitting a desire to leave feels like betrayal—of patients, colleagues, or one's younger self. So the thoughts stay private. You continue to show up, function, and appear "fine," while internally rehearsing the idea of an exit she does not yet feel permitted to take.

This internal conflict accelerates burnout rather than resolving it.

ASC vs Hospital Nuance

In ASCs, exit fantasies often revolve around:

- Leaving healthcare entirely
- Seeking work with clearer boundaries
- Escaping productivity pressure disguised as "efficiency."

You feel competent but exploited.

In hospitals, fantasies often center on:

- Non-bedside roles
- Positions without constant vigilance or emotional exposure
- Work that ends when the shift ends

You still believe in patient care, but no longer in the system delivering it. In both cases, burnout has eroded the belief that this role is sustainable.

The Psychological Cost of Suppressing Exit Fantasies

When nurses ignore or suppress these thoughts, burnout deepens. Instead of prompting change, the fantasies coexist with continued over-functioning. You stay—but with:

- Reduced emotional engagement
- Increased cynicism
- Minimal investment beyond what is required

This is often misinterpreted as laziness or disengagement. In reality, it is self-protection after prolonged depletion.

The Warning Sign Burnout Makes Inevitable

Quiet exit fantasies are not a failure of resilience. They are evidence that resilience has been overused.

They signal:

- The workload exceeds recovery capacity
- Emotional labor has gone unrecognized

- Your identity has narrowed too far around work

By the time these thoughts become frequent, burnout is no longer emerging—it is established.

Reframing the Exit Fantasy

The goal is not immediate departure. The goal is to listen to what the fantasy is communicating. Often, it is not saying: "I want to stop being a nurse." It is saying: "I cannot continue under these conditions." When recognized early, exit fantasies can serve as leverage for boundary-setting, role redesign, or structural change. When ignored, they lead to abrupt resignation, health decline, or emotional shutdown.

6

WHY NURSES LEAVE —
AND WHAT THEY MOVE
TOWARD IN HEALTHCARE

LEAVING BEDSIDE, NOT HEALTHCARE

Many nurses do not want to abandon healthcare —they want to leave constant vigilance, emotional exposure, and unsustainable responsibility. Burned-out nurses do not need vague encouragement. They need a lower emotional load, clearer boundaries, and realistic options that respect their training and experience.

WHY ASC CAREER LADDERS LOOK FLAT

AMBULATORY SURGERY CENTERS ARE BUILT TO BE LEAN. THAT EFFICIENCY IS THEIR STRENGTH—AND ALSO THE REASON TRADITIONAL NURSING LADDERS DON'T EXIST INSIDE THEM.

MOST ASCS ARE DESIGNED AROUND THREE LAYERS:

- An administrator

- A clinical lead or head nurse
- Staff nurses who carry the operational and clinical load

There is no utilization department. There is no quality office. There is no documentation improvement team down the hall. Not because those functions don't matter—but because they are handled **outside** the building, at the system, network, or vendor level. This creates a quiet problem for experienced ASC nurses: they grow, but the building does not. So when ASC nurses transition, they do not "move up" internally. They **move outward**, carrying their expertise into roles that exist beyond the center's walls. That is not stagnation. That is how ambulatory careers are structured.

WHAT ASC STAFF NURSES CAN REALISTICALLY TRANSITION TO

This list assumes:

- Small to mid-size ASCs
- Limited internal hierarchy
- No formal non-bedside departments

The focus is portable roles, not internal promotions. ASC transitions usually share three characteristics:

- A new employer (health system, network, vendor, or consulting group)
- A shift in responsibility (from moment-to-moment execution to planning, coordination, or education)
- A change in emotional load, even when clinical knowledge remains central

HERE ARE SOME EXAMPLES
OF TRANSITION ROLES:

1. Pre-Admission Testing

For many ASC nurses, Pre-Admission Testing (PAT) is the first role that feels familiar without being overwhelming. It uses the same clinical judgment nurses rely on at the bedside, but relocates it to a point where it can be effective—**before the day of surgery begins**. PAT does not replace surgeons or anesthesia. It does not make final decisions. What it does is change timing, and timing changes everything.

What PAT Nurses Actually Do. In a PAT role, nurses review patients days or weeks before surgery rather than minutes before wheels-in. The work is deliberate and structured.

PAT nurses typically:

- Review medical histories, labs, imaging, and consults

- Identify missing information or incomplete clearances
- Screen for guideline-based risk factors
- Document findings clearly and consistently
- Escalate concerns through defined pathways to anesthesia or surgical teams

The authority is procedural, not hierarchical. PAT nurses do not cancel cases. They ensure that concerns are visible, documented, and addressed early enough to be effective.

How This Differs From ASC Floor Nursing

ASC staff nurses are used to discovering problems under pressure. A patient arrives with incomplete testing. A clearance is missing. A comorbidity raises concern. The nurse sees the issue, but the schedule is already moving, and the patient is already anxious. The problem becomes a scramble rather than a discussion.

In PAT, the same issues surface without urgency.
There is time to:

- Clarify
- Document
- Escalate appropriately
- Allow decision-makers to respond

Instead of absorbing the consequences of late discoveries, the nurse prevents them from becoming day-of-surgery crises.

What Changes Emotionally

The most significant change is not the work itself—it is the emotional load attached to it. At the ASC bedside, nurses often carry responsibility without authority. They see risks they cannot resolve and then absorb patient frustration, provider irritation, and schedule pressure when those risks surface late.

In PAT:

- Responsibility is shared
- Concerns are formalized
- Escalation is expected, not disruptive

The nurse is no longer the emotional buffer between the patient and the system. The work still matters—but it does not follow the nurse home.

Example

An ASC nurse who previously thought, "This should have been addressed earlier," now encounters the same issue during a chart review days before surgery. She identifies the concern, documents it, and escalates it through the appropriate pathway. Anesthesia or the surgeon reviews it with time to act. The nurse does not decide the outcome. She ensures that the issue is identified early enough to enable a rational decision. That difference alone removes much of the day-of-surgery stress ASC nurses are accustomed to carrying.

Why PAT Works for Burned-Out ASC Nurses

PAT appeals to nurses who:

- Trust their clinical judgment

- Are tired of reacting to preventable problems
- Want to use experience without physical strain
- Need clearer boundaries around responsibility

The role rewards attentiveness and follow-through, not speed or endurance. Many nurses describe the shift as moving from constant vigilance to a more contained responsibility.

What PAT Is Not

PAT is not:

- A promotion into authority
- A decision-making role
- A way to control scheduling

It is a protective role for patients, providers, and nurses alike. PAT is not about doing less. It is about doing the same careful, experienced work before urgency distorts it. For ASC nurses who feel trapped between responsibility and powerlessness, PAT offers something rare in ambulatory care: Time, structure, and the ability to put the day away when it ends.

Why This Role Often Comes With a New Employer: Most ASCs do not operate PAT internally. These roles are typically housed within:

- Hospital systems
- Surgical networks
- Pre-operative clinics
- Centralized scheduling or assessment teams

For ASC nurses, transitioning into PAT usually means leaving the center—not leaving healthcare.

2. SURGICAL SERVICES COORDINATOR

For ASC staff nurses who have spent years holding together days that were never realistically designed, the Surgical Services Coordinator role represents a fundamental shift: from absorbing dysfunction to shaping structure. This role exists almost exclusively at the system, network, or ASC-management level, not within a single center. It is designed to solve problems that no individual ASC can fix alone. Surgical Services Coordinators do not run the day-to-day operation of a center. They control the framework within which centers operate.

1. Standardized Workflows

ASC nurses recognize the significant variation across surgeons, sites, and teams. Coordinators are responsible for reducing unnecessary variation that creates friction.
   They may:

- Define standard pre-op, intra-op, and post-op workflows

- Align turnover expectations across sites
- Clarify handoff processes
- Reduce "special rules" that only one surgeon follows

The goal is not perfection—it is **predictability**. Instead of every center reinventing the wheel, the coordinator ensures that core processes function the same way wherever possible.

2. Policy Alignment Across Sites

In multicenter organizations, policies often exist but are interpreted differently across sites.
Coordinators:

- Review how policies are actually being applied
- Identify inconsistencies that create risk or confusion
- Clarify expectations so staff are not caught between "policy" and "practice."

This matters because ASC nurses are often the ones blamed when policy ambiguity surfaces in real time. Policy alignment protects staff from being put in impossible positions.

3. Communication Structures

Much of what appears to be chaos in ASCs is actually a communication failure.
Coordinators design and maintain:

- Clear lines of communication between centers and leadership
- Defined points of contact for issues
- Consistent messaging to surgeons and anesthesia groups

Instead of nurses negotiating the same issues repeatedly, communication becomes institutional rather than personal.

4. Escalation Pathways

One of the most meaningful controls in this role is formal escalation.

Coordinators define:

- What issues require escalation
- Who they escalate to
- How quickly responses are expected
- How decisions are documented

This removes the burden from individual nurses to decide when "something is serious enough" to push back. Escalation becomes a process, not a confrontation.

What Surgical Services Coordinators DO NOT Control

This role does **not** magically remove all frustration. Understanding its limits is essential.

1. Individual Surgeon Behavior

Coordinators cannot:

- Change personalities
- Enforce compliance single-handedly
- Override clinical autonomy

They work through structure and expectation, not authority. Surgeon behavior improves when systems make expectations clear—not because someone tells them to behave differently.

2. Daily Staffing Ratios

Staffing decisions are typically made at:

- The center level
- The administrative level

Coordinators may identify staffing risks or trends, but they do not assign staff on a day-to-day basis. This is intentional. The role is strategic rather than operational.

3. Case Volume Decisions

Coordinators do not control:

- How many cases are booked
- Block allocations
- Revenue-driven scheduling

Those decisions sit with leadership and surgeons. What coordinators can do is make the consequences of heavy scheduling visible, so nurses aren't the only ones feeling the strain when volume gets pushed too far.

How This Role Actually Feels to Nurses

For nurses transitioning from ASC staff roles, the most significant emotional shift is: "I'm no longer the person apologizing for a broken system." Instead of managing frustration in real time, the nurse works on the conditions that create it. The responsibility is still real—but it is distributed, documented, and shared.

Who This Role Fits Best

This role tends to fit ASC nurses who:

- Notice patterns quickly
- Are frustrated by repeated problems more than individual crises
- Are respected for judgment, not speed
- Want influence without physical strain

It does **not** fit nurses who want:

- Direct control over daily operations
- Immediate visible results
- Clear authority over individuals

Progress here is incremental rather than dramatic.

Surgical Services Coordinators do not "fix ASCs." **They** reduce how often nurses are forced to compensate for system gaps. For ASC staff nurses who are tired of being the glue, this role offers something rare: the chance to design the structure rather than hold it together.

3. CLINICAL LIAISON /
PHYSICIAN PRACTICE LIAISON

For ASC staff nurses, this role often feels familiar long before it has a name. Many have already been doing pieces of it informally—returning calls, clarifying expectations, smoothing misunderstandings, and translating reality between the center and physician offices. The liaison role formalizes work that nurses have carried out for years.

What These Roles Actually Do

Clinical liaisons operate at the boundary between physician practices and surgical facilities. Their primary responsibility is not enforcement, but alignment.

Educate Physician Offices

Liaisons ensure offices understand:

- ASC processes and requirements
- Pre-op expectations
- Documentation standards
- Timing realities

This education is ongoing, not one-time. Practices change

staff frequently, and expectations drift unless they are reinforced. The liaison becomes the consistent point of reference.

Align Expectations

Much ASC friction comes from mismatched assumptions:

- What "ready for surgery" means
- What information is required and when
- What can realistically be accommodated

Liaisons help set expectations early, so nurses are not left
explaining or apologizing later. Instead of correcting problems after they arrive, the liaison works to prevent predictable
misunderstandings.

Communicate Requirements

Liaisons clarify what is required—not as a personal
demand, but as a system reality. This relieves pressure on
bedside nurses, who are often expected to explain or defend
rules they did not create.

The message shifts from: "The nurse says we need this."
to: "This is how the system works."

Identify Recurring Disconnects

Because liaisons see patterns across multiple practices
and centers, they are often the first to notice:

- The same missing information
- The same late changes
- The same points of confusion

Rather than addressing each issue in isolation, they flag
trends and work with leadership to correct them at the source.

What These Roles Do *Not* Do

This role has influence, not authority.
Clinical liaisons **do not**:

- Enforce compliance
- Override clinical decisions
- Control scheduling or case volume
- Discipline practices or providers

Understanding these limits is critical. Nurses who enter this role expecting command-and-control will be frustrated quickly. The power here is relational and structural, not hierarchical.

How This Role Actually Feels to Nurses

For ASC nurses, the emotional shift is subtle but meaningful.

At the bedside, nurses often absorb frustration they did not cause:

- Patients arrive unprepared
- Offices send incomplete information
- Surgeons express dissatisfaction

In the liaison role, the nurse is no longer the final point of contact for those frustrations. Instead of reacting to problems, she works before they become problems.

Who This Role Fits Best

This role tends to suit ASC nurses who:

- Communicate clearly and calmly
- Notice patterns across people and systems
- Are respected for professionalism and credibility
- Prefer prevention over reaction

It is less satisfying for nurses who want:

- Direct authority

- Immediate visible outcomes
- Control over daily operations

Progress here is measured in fewer bad days, not dramatic wins. For ASC nurses tired of being the point where every disconnect finally explodes, this role offers a way to use experience and voice—without carrying the emotional fallout personally.

Where Nurses Find Clinical Liaison / Physician Practice Liaison Jobs

1. Health Systems & Hospital Networks
(Most common and most stable source)
Large systems employ nurses whose job is to:

- Interface with physician offices
- Align outpatient practices with system requirements
- Reduce downstream disruption to ASCs and hospitals

These roles are often listed under titles like:

- Clinical Liaison
- Physician Relations Nurse
- Provider Engagement Specialist
- Practice Integration Nurse

They usually sit in:

- Surgical services
- Physician relations

- Network operations

Where to look:
Health system career pages (not just "Nursing" sections).
ASC Management Companies
Large ASC groups employ nurses to support **multiple centers and practices**.
These roles focus on:

- Standardizing expectations
- Educating practices
- Reducing friction across sites

Job titles may include:

- Clinical Liaison
- Surgical Services Liaison
- Practice Relations Nurse
- Regional Clinical Support

4. PHYSICIAN PRACTICE MANAGEMENT & MSOS

(MANAGEMENT SERVICES ORGANIZATIONS)

Many ASC nurses have never heard of MSOs, even though MSOs quietly shape much of what makes—or breaks—their day. MSOs are organizations that **run the business and operational side of physician practices**, allowing physicians to focus on clinical care. They sit between physician offices, ASCs, hospitals, and payers, coordinating how work actually flows. For ASC nurses seeking to transition, MSOs are among the **most realistic and underutilized pathways**.

What MSOs Actually Need From Nurses

MSOs do not hire nurses to provide bedside care. They hire nurses to bring clinical realism into operational decisions that are otherwise made by non-clinical staff.

Specifically, nurses are hired to:

Align Practices With Surgical Facilities

Physician offices and ASCs often operate with mismatched assumptions:

- What documentation is required
- What "ready for surgery" means
- How timelines actually work

MSO nurses help practices understand ASC requirements early, so problems don't surface at the last minute and land on staff nurses. The goal is not enforcement—it is alignment.

Improve Operational Readiness

Operational readiness means:

- Charts are complete
- Clearances are appropriate
- Patients are prepared
- Schedules are realistic

ASC nurses already know exactly what happens when readiness fails. MSOs hire nurses to prevent that failure before cases are assigned to the schedule. This work is proactive, repetitive, and pattern-based—not crisis-driven.

Reduce Scheduling and Documentation Issues

Most scheduling problems are not one-offs. They are **systemic**:

- The same offices submit incomplete information
- The same requirements are misunderstood
- The same last-minute changes occur

MSO nurses identify these patterns and work with practices to correct them at the source. Instead of nurses on the floor absorbing the fallout, the system absorbs it upstream.

Why These Roles Are Rarely Nursing-Branded

MSOs are operational organizations, not clinical ones. As a result, job titles rarely include the word *nurse*, even when nursing experience is essential.

Common titles include:

- Practice Operations Specialist

- Clinical Integration Specialist
- Provider Relations Specialist
- Practice Transformation Consultant
- Operations Manager (Clinical Background Required)

Nurses often overlook these roles because they don't "sound like nursing," even though the work depends heavily on nursing judgment.

What These Roles Do *Not* Do

To be clear, MSO nurses:

- Do not discipline practices
- Do not override physician decisions
- Do not control case volume
- Do not enforce compliance independently

They work through education, structure, and relationship, not authority. Their value lies in credibility and consistency, not command.

How This Role Actually Feels to ASC Nurses

For many ASC nurses, this is the first role where:

- Their experience is respected without urgency
- Problems are addressed before they explode
- Responsibility exists without constant pressure

The nurse is no longer the last stop when something goes wrong. She is part of the system that prevents predictable breakdowns.

A Realistic Example

An ASC nurse knows that incomplete documentation from certain practices leads to delayed starts, frustrated patients, and staff scrambling.

In an MSO role, she:

- Notices the pattern
- Works with the practice to clarify expectations
- Helps standardize submissions
- Reduces repeat issues over time

She does not control the practice, but she changes how often the problem occurs.

Where to Look (Practically)

When searching job boards or websites, nurses should **not** search for "nurse."

Instead, look under:

- Operations
- Integration
- Provider relations
- Practice management
- Network operations

Keywords that signal an MSO role:

- "Practice alignment"
- "Clinical integration"
- "Operational readiness"
- "Physician practice support"

These roles are often hybrid or remote and may serve multiple practices or centers.

5. MEDICAL DEVICE & PROCEDURE-FOCUSED COMPANIES

Many ASC nurses assume that working for a device or procedure-focused company means selling. In reality, most reputable vendors maintain non-sales clinical roles because their products only succeed when used correctly, safely, and consistently. These roles exist to protect outcomes—not quotas.

Why These Companies Hire Nurses

Device and procedure companies operate in real clinical environments, not theory. They need people who understand:

- How cases actually run
- Where workflows break down
- What staff can realistically absorb
- How small changes affect the whole day

ASC nurses already know this. These companies hire nurses to bring **clinical reality** into education, implementation, and ongoing support—roles that require credibility, not persuasion.

Common Nurse-Focused Roles (What They Really Are)

Clinical Liaison (Vendor-Side)

This role focuses on supporting facilities and practices that use a specific device or procedure.

The nurse:

- Serves as the clinical point of contact
- Helps practices understand best-use standards
- Supports adoption without managing cases

This is not a sales role. The liaison does not negotiate contracts or quotas. Their credibility comes from clinical knowledge, not persuasion.

Clinical Education Specialist

Education specialists train staff before, during, and after implementation.

They may:

- Educate nurses and techs on device use
- Support onboarding for new staff
- Reinforce safety protocols and workflow integration

The work is structured and repeatable. Teaching replaces urgency. ASC nurses often thrive here because they already train informally—this role **formalizes that expertise**.

Practice Support Nurse

Practice support nurses focus on helping facilities integrate devices or procedures into daily operations.

They may:

- Assist with workflow alignment
- Help adapt protocols to real-world settings
- Identify recurring use issues and address them

This role is ongoing, relationship-based, and preventive.

What These Roles Actually Involve

Across all three titles, the core responsibilities are consistent:

- Educating practices
- Ensuring staff understand not just *how* to use a product, but *why* it's used a certain way.
- Supporting workflow alignment
- Assisting facilities in integrating new tools without disrupting workflow or safety.
- Serving as a clinical bridge
- Translating between clinical staff and corporate teams—without being a salesperson.

What These Roles Do *Not* Involve

These roles do **not**:

- Carry sales quotas
- Close deals
- Negotiate pricing
- Push product volume

If a posting emphasizes commissions, targets, or revenue generation, it is **not** this role. ASC nurses should be cautious of titles that blur education with sales.

How This Role Feels Compared to ASC Nursing (Besides better pay)

For ASC nurses, the most significant shift is in pace and proximity.

Instead of:

- Running rooms

- Managing turnover
- Absorbing schedule pressure

They are:

- Teaching
- Advising
- Supporting integration

The responsibility is real—but **bounded**. Many nurses describe the shift as: "I'm still in healthcare, but I'm no longer carrying the day on my shoulders."

Why ASC Nurses Are Strong Fits

ASC nurses bring:

- Procedural fluency
- Realistic workflow judgment
- Credibility with staff
- Comfort teaching peers. Vendors value nurses who can say: "Here's how this actually works in a real ASC." That honesty prevents problems and builds trust.

Where to Look (Practically)

These roles are rarely posted under "Nursing."
ASC nurses should look at:

- Vendor career pages
- Medical device company websites

Search under:

- Clinical

- Education
- Implementation
- Practice Support

Key terms to watch for:

- "Clinical Education"
- "Implementation Specialist"
- "Practice Support"
- "Clinical Liaison (Non-Sales)"

LinkedIn is especially useful, as many of these roles are filled through professional networks.

A Realistic Caution

These roles often involve:

- Regional travel
- Periods of intense onboarding support
- Independence and self-direction

They suit nurses who value autonomy and teaching more than routine.

They frustrate nurses who want:

- Fixed locations
- Predictable daily schedules
- Minimal travel

6. JOB BOARDS (WITH THE RIGHT SEARCH TERMS)

Most nurses miss these roles because they search for **"ASC nurse"** or **"OR nurse."**

Better search terms include:

- "Clinical Liaison"
- "Physician Liaison"
- "Provider Relations"
- "Practice Integration"
- "Clinical Integration Nurse"

Best platforms:

- LinkedIn
- Indeed (advanced filters)
- Health system job portals

LinkedIn is particularly important because many of these roles are **network-hired and** not widely advertised.

7. AMBULATORY QUALITY OR COMPLIANCE ROLES

For ASCs, accreditation and compliance are not optional—they are existential. One failed survey, one unresolved deficiency, or one pattern of noncompliance can shut a center down. That reality is why quality and compliance roles rarely sit inside a single ASC. They operate at the network, management, or consulting level, supporting multiple centers simultaneously. For ASC nurses, this is one of the most direct skill translations available.

Why This Role Fits ASC Nurses

ASC nurses already operate in a compliance-driven environment.

They live in:
Policies that change frequently

- Checklists that must be followed precisely
- Survey readiness that never entirely turns off

They understand what happens when standards are unclear or inconsistently applied—and they are often the ones quietly fixing gaps before anyone else notices. Quality and compliance roles formalize this work. Rather than being responsible for "doing it right" in a single center, the nurse helps ensure that multiple centers consistently meet standards.

What These Roles Actually Do

Ambulatory quality and compliance nurses focus on prevention, visibility, and consistency, not discipline.

They typically:

- Conduct chart audits and process reviews
- Assess compliance with accreditation standards
- Identify risk patterns across centers
- Help centers prepare for surveys
- Recommend corrective actions and standardization

They do not enforce policy by punishment. They make risk visible and hard to ignore.

What These Roles Do *Not* Do

Quality and compliance nurses do not:

- Run daily operations
- Discipline staff
- Override administrators
- Make staffing decisions

They work through assessment, education, and reporting, not authority. This distinction matters. Nurses who enter these roles expecting control will be frustrated. Nurses who value clarity and influence will thrive.

Typical Employers

Individual ASCs rarely post these roles. They are usually employed by:

- ASC chains overseeing multiple centers
- ASC management companies
- Healthcare consulting firms specializing in ambulatory care
- Accreditation support organizations

Job titles vary widely and often omit the word *nurse*:

- Ambulatory Quality Specialist
- Compliance Analyst
- Clinical Quality Consultant
- Survey Readiness Coordinator

ASC nurses often overlook these postings because they are listed under quality, compliance, or operations rather than nursing.

How This Role Actually Feels

For many ASC nurses, the emotional shift is immediate. At the bedside, safety feels fragile and personal. One missed step can have immediate consequences.

In a quality or compliance role:

- Responsibility is shared
- Risk is addressed proactively
- Problems are surfaced before they harm patients or staff

The nurse is no longer reacting in the moment. She is protecting systems.

A Realistic Example

An ASC nurse knows which policies are followed only "when surveyors are coming."

In a quality role, she:

- Identifies the pattern
- Works with leadership to standardize practice
- Helps centers close gaps before they become citations

She does not shame staff. She builds consistency.

Who This Role Fits Best

This role suits ASC nurses who:

- Are detail-oriented
- Think in patterns rather than moments
- Prefer prevention to crisis management
- Are comfortable giving feedback diplomatically

It frustrates nurses who want:

- Immediate visible results
- Direct control over daily operations
- Hands-on patient care

7

CROSSING THE LINE

What changes when you move between a hospital and
an ASC

When nurses move between hospitals and ASCs,
they often believe they are changing pace or
schedule, or simply seeking a change. What
they are actually changing is **structure** — and structure
shapes everything: power, visibility, protection, and consequence. Hospitals and ASCs are not just different workplaces.
They are fundamentally different systems. Understanding that
difference is what determines whether a transition feels stabilizing or disorienting.

Scale changes how risk is absorbed.

Hospitals are built for volume. They rely on redundancy:
multiple units, layers of leadership, float pools, rapid
response teams, committees, and policies designed to
distribute responsibility across the system. When something
goes wrong, the impact is absorbed broadly. Accountability

exists, but it is diffused. A nurse can have a difficult interaction, document thoroughly, give a report, and move on. The system holds the weight.

ASCs operate on the opposite principle. They are intentionally lean. Teams are small. Coverage is tight. When something goes wrong, it is felt immediately and personally. There is little distance between action and consequence. One decision can alter the entire day. Going from a hospital to a one-doctor ASC is a radical shift. Neither structure is superior. But they place very different demands on the nurse.

Visibility Is the Hidden Variable

In hospitals, visibility is diluted. You are one of many nurses, often caring for multiple patients across shifts. Interactions are frequent but brief. Memory is short because the system is large. In ASCs, visibility is concentrated. You work repeatedly with the same surgeons, anesthesiologists, administrators, and staff. Your communication style, confidence, and response to pressure are noticed. There is no anonymity. Patterns form quickly. This can feel empowering to nurses who value autonomy and consistency. It can feel exposing to those accustomed to blending into the larger flow of a hospital. Visibility amplifies both strengths and missteps.

Power Operates Differently

Hospitals rely on formal authority. Titles, policies, and escalation pathways matter. Power is distributed through organizational charts, committees, and governance structures. When conflict arises, there are defined routes for resolution.

ASCs rely heavily on informal authority. Power often flows toward those who control volume, revenue, or specialized expertise. Influence is exercised in real time, not through committees. Decisions are usually negotiated rather than delegated. For nurses, this shift can be jarring. In hospitals, protection comes from process. In ASCs, protection comes from understanding, consistency, and relationships.

The Cost of Flexibility

ASCs are often praised for their flexibility. Decisions are made quickly. Changes happen fast. Schedules adapt. That flexibility can be liberating — until it isn't. Without strong consistency, flexibility becomes unpredictability. Nurses may not know whether standards will be enforced or negotiated. Boundaries may shift depending on who is present or how the day is going. Hospitals are slower to change, but that slowness provides a buffer. Rules may be frustrating, but they are also stabilizing. The same feature that makes ASCs appealing can also make them destabilizing if leadership is inconsistent.

Emotional Labor Takes Different Forms

Hospital nursing often involves sustained emotional exposure to patients and families. The emotional load comes from acuity, volume, and moral distress. ASC nursing involves concentrated interpersonal dynamics. The emotional load comes from close working relationships, repeated interactions with the same personalities, and high expectations for smooth performance. In hospitals, emotional fatigue is cumulative. In ASCs, it is often sharp and relational. Both forms are real. They exhaust different parts of you.

Why Nurses Misjudge the Transition

Most nurses underestimate this structural shift because they focus on surface differences: hours, patient mix, physical pace. Those matters are important, but they are not what destabilize people. What destabilizes nurses is moving from a system that absorbs risk to one that reflects it immediately. From anonymity to visibility. From formal authority to informal influence. When nurses understand this before they move, the transition becomes manageable. When they don't, they often assume something is wrong with them. It isn't.

What This Means Going Forward

This structural difference explains why some nurses feel relief after switching — and others feel exposed. It explains why the same nurse can feel confident in one environment and unsure in another. The environment didn't change their competence.

It changed the system around them. Recognizing that distinction is the first step toward moving intentionally rather than reactively and toward choosing environments that support not only your schedule but also your stability.

HOSPITAL → ASC

WHY NURSES LEAVE—AND WHAT THEY OFTEN DON'T EXPECT

For many hospital nurses, moving to an ASC feels like a strategic escape. The decision is rarely impulsive. It typically follows years of rotating shifts, chronic understaffing, emotional overload, and a sense that the system will never stabilize. The ASC represents something different: predictability, control, and relief. In many ways, that promise is real. But it is incomplete.

Why Hospital Nurses Choose ASCs

Hospital nurses who move to ASCs often seek fewer uncertainties. They want schedules that don't change weekly, patients who are not critically unstable, and a pace that feels manageable rather than relentless. They are tired of being stretched thin across too many rooms, too many patients, and too many competing demands. Burnout occurs. ASCs offer shorter days, fewer nights and weekends, and a narrower scope of care. The work is more procedural, the patient population is healthier, and the daily rhythm is more predictable. For nurses who have lived in constant hospital chaos, this can feel like regaining control over their lives. Not that ASCs don't have their fair share. What they are really seeking is containment.

Many hospital nurses assume that fewer patients automatically means less stress. What they discover instead is that stress changes shape. It becomes interpersonal rather than systemic. Instead of absorbing volume, you absorb proximity. Instead of managing many brief interactions, you manage fewer but more repeated ones. The required skill set differs, even when the clinical work feels familiar.

What Changes Immediately

The first shift in an ASC often feels deceptively calm. The environment is quieter. The patient flow is more precise. The work feels more focused. But underneath that calm, the structure has changed completely. In an ASC, there are fewer people to absorb tension. Fewer layers of leadership. Fewer buffers between decision-making and consequence. Interactions that would be diluted in a hospital are concentrated here. Hospital nurses are used to escalation pathways: charge nurse, unit manager, supervisor, and risk management. In an ASC, escalation is often direct. The administrator is nearby. The surgeon is in the room. Decisions happen face-to-face, sometimes in real time. Hospital nurses are accustomed to decisions being distributed across roles and time. In ASCs, decisions compress. Fewer people are involved, and fewer layers exist between choice and consequence. A decision made in the morning can shape the entire day. A comment made in passing can have unintended consequences.

This compression is not inherently negative. It simply requires a different level of intentionality. Nurses who adjust quickly learn to slow themselves internally even when the environment feels faster externally. Those who don't may feel exposed, even when nothing overtly goes wrong.

The Visibility Shift

One of the most underestimated changes is visibility. In small environments, patterns form rapidly. Reliability is noticed. Inconsistency is noticed faster. There is little room to reset impressions through anonymity. This does not mean you must perform constantly. It implies that steadiness becomes more valuable than intensity. Hospital nurses who succeed in ASCs learn that how they recover from pressure matters more than how they avoid it. A single moment of strain is rarely damaging. Repeated unpredictability is. In a hospital, you can have an off day and still function within the system. In an ASC, patterns form quickly. Communication style, response to pressure, and emotional regulation are noticed. You work with the same people repeatedly, often in close quarters. This level of visibility rewards consistency and clarity. It can also magnify discomfort. A single tense interaction can linger longer because there is no crowd to disappear into. Hospital nurses often underestimate the importance of relational skills in small settings. Technical competence is assumed. What stands out is how you navigate pressure.

Power Feels Different — and More Personal

One of the most important adjustments hospital nurses must make is separating personal worth from perceived influence. In hospitals, authority feels structural. In ASCs, influence feels relational. When decisions don't land the way a nurse expects, it can feel personal — even when it isn't. Nurses who struggle most are often those who assume that fairness operates identically across systems. In reality, ASCs rely more heavily on informal authority. Learning to see that dynamic clearly prevents unnecessary self-doubt and over-accommodation.

In hospitals, power is formal and procedural. Policies matter. Documentation protects you. Authority flows through defined channels. In ASCs, power is often informal and situational. Influence may be tied to case volume, specialty, or long-standing relationships. Surgeons are not just providers; they are often economic drivers of the center. That reality shapes how decisions are made, even when no one states it explicitly. Hospital nurses may expect institutional backing to feel the same. When it doesn't, they may mistake structural differences for personal vulnerability. It isn't a lack of support. It's a different kind of system.

The Emotional Shift Nobody Warns You About

Hospital nursing is exhausted through volume and acuity. ASC nursing exhausts through proximity. You may have fewer patients, but you interact more deeply and repeatedly with the same team. Tension does not dissipate into the next shift or unit. It stays in the room. This is why some hospital nurses experience unexpected fatigue in ASCs. The work is physically lighter, but emotionally sharper. You are not managing a constant crisis; you are managing a continual relationship.

Where Hospital Nurses Struggle Most

Hospital nurses transitioning to ASCs often struggle when they:

- Expect policies to buffer interpersonal conflict
- Assume escalation will feel neutral rather than personal
- Over-accommodate to avoid standing out
- Underestimate the impact of surgeon dynamics
- Interpret inconsistency as personal failure rather than structural reality

These struggles are not about competence. They concern misalignment between expectations and the environment.

What Makes the Transition Successful

Hospital nurses who thrive in ASCs tend to adjust how they operate. They become more intentional in communication. They learn the informal power map early. They stop expecting anonymity and start cultivating steadiness. They recognize that consistency matters more than intensity. That calm authority travels further than volume. And those boundaries, when applied predictably, protect relationships rather than damage them. The ASC does not reward the nurse who quietly absorbs chaos. It rewards the nurse who navigates it clearly.

The Core Lesson of the Transition

Moving from a hospital to an ASC does not mean leaving stress behind. It means trading one kind of pressure for another. The nurses who feel relief are not the ones who escape difficulty. They understand the nature of the difficulty they are facing and adjust accordingly. When that adjustment occurs intentionally, the ASC becomes not only easier but

also sustainable. Hospital nurses who adapt most smoothly
tend to do three things early:

1. They observe before asserting.

   2. They ask clarifying questions instead of assuming
support will appear automatically.

   3. And they establish consistent communication patterns
rather than relying on intensity or urgency.

   These choices do not immediately make the work easier.
They make it sustainable.

ASC → HOSPITAL

For nurses working in ASCs, moving to a hospital is rarely about ambition. It is usually about relief. After time in an ASC, some nurses begin to feel exposed. The smallness that once felt efficient starts to feel constricting. Interpersonal tension carries more weight. Power feels concentrated. The margin for error — relational or operational — feels thin. The hospital begins to appear protective. In many ways, it is.

Why ASC Nurses Choose Hospitals

ASC nurses who move to hospitals often seek structure. They want clearer escalation pathways, formal policies, and systems that do not hinge on individual personalities. They are tired of negotiating boundaries one interaction at a time. The relief ASC nurses feel when contemplating a hospital move is often emotional before it is practical. It is the relief of distance — from constant visibility, from repeated interpersonal friction, from feeling personally exposed to every decision. What they sometimes underestimate is that distance also dilutes control. The same structures that protect also slow.

The same policies that buffer also constrain. Understanding this tradeoff prevents frustration from turning inward.

Hospitals offer something ASCs cannot: institutional insulation. There are committees, managers, supervisors, and risk departments. Decisions are documented, not improvised. Conflict can be escalated without confronting the same person the next day. For nurses who have felt the constant pressure of visibility, this distance feels stabilizing. The relief ASC nurses feel when contemplating a hospital move is often emotional before it is practical. It is the relief of distance — from constant visibility, from repeated interpersonal friction, from feeling personally exposed to every decision. What they sometimes underestimate is that distance also dilutes influence. The same structures that protect also slow. The same policies that buffer also constrain. Understanding this tradeoff prevents frustration from turning inward.

What Changes Immediately

The first weeks in a hospital often feel overwhelming in a different way. The pace is faster. Patient acuity is higher. Staffing ratios are heavier. Emotional exposure increases. The structure that protects also slows. Decisions take longer. Systems are rigid. Problems that would be addressed immediately in an ASC may linger in hospitals for weeks or months. ASC nurses often underestimate the extent of the autonomy they've developed. In hospitals, autonomy is constrained by policy, staffing grids, and the chain of command. The ability to make quick operational decisions is replaced by documentation and escalation. The tradeoff is protection for control. ASC nurses are often surprised by the limited control they have over the pace of care in hospitals. In ASCs, flow is actively managed. In hospitals, flow is endured. Bottlenecks are absorbed rather than resolved. Nurses who struggle most are those who attempt to recreate ASC efficiency inside hospital systems. Nurses who adapt learn to redirect their strengths — from speed to vigilance, from immediate correction to documentation and escalation.

The Loss of Personal Influence

In an ASC, individual nurses often have outsized influence. Their reliability, communication, and experience shape daily operations. Leadership knows them personally. In a hospital, that influence diffuses. You become part of a larger workforce. Your voice still matters, but it competes with many others. Decisions are less relational and more procedural. For some nurses, this feels like relief. For others, it feels like invisibility. For ASC nurses accustomed to being known, the anonymity of hospitals can feel like erasure. But invisibility is not always disempowerment. In hospitals, anonymity can also be protection. Nurses who thrive learn to use systems rather than resist them. They stop expecting recognition through proximity and begin deliberately leveraging structure. Influence shifts from presence to process.

For ASC nurses accustomed to being known, the anonymity of hospitals can feel like erasure. But invisibility is not always disempowerment. In hospitals, anonymity can also be protection.

Nurses who thrive learn to use systems rather than resist them. They stop expecting recognition through proximity and begin deliberately leveraging structure. Influence shifts from presence to process.

The Emotional Weight Shifts Again

ASC nursing focuses on emotional stress related to relationships. Hospital nursing distributes emotional stress across patients, families, and outcomes. In hospitals, patients are carried longer. You see deterioration, loss, and moral distress more frequently. You may leave one shift knowing you did everything possible, and still feel it wasn't enough. ASC nurses moving to hospitals often underestimate the emotional endurance required by hospital work. The distance from surgeon dynamics is replaced by proximity to the patient suffering. Hospital nursing requires a different kind of emotional endurance. Outcomes unfold slowly. Closure is rare. Emotional labor is not concentrated in a few relationships but is distributed across many patients and families. Nurses moving from ASCs to hospitals must rebuild boundaries that protect against prolonged exposure. What once felt distant may now feel heavy. Awareness prevents compassion from becoming depleted.

Hospital nursing requires a different kind of emotional endurance. Outcomes unfold slowly. Closure is rare. Emotional labor is not concentrated in a few relationships but distributed across many patients and families. Nurses moving from ASCs to hospitals must rebuild boundaries to protect against prolonged exposure. What once felt distant may now feel heavy. Awareness prevents compassion from becoming depleted.

Where ASC Nurses Struggle Most

ASC nurses moving to hospitals often struggle when they:

- Expect escalation to result in quick resolution
- Feel frustrated by bureaucratic delay
- Miss the autonomy of small-team decision-making

- Underestimate patient complexity
- Struggle with being one voice among many

These struggles are not about skill. They are about **scale**.

What Helps the Transition

ASC nurses who adapt well to hospitals reframe the structure's offerings. They prioritize documentation as protection rather than a burden. They adjust expectations about speed. They rebuild emotional boundaries for prolonged patient exposure. They stop expecting personal influence and start using the process intentionally. The hospital rewards nurses who can operate within systems — not around them.

The Core Lesson of Moving

Moving from an ASC to a hospital does not constitute a step backward. It means choosing a different kind of containment. Hospitals provide insulation at the cost of agility. ASCs provide autonomy at the expense of exposure. Neither is inherently safer or harder; they simply distribute pressure differently. The nurses who feel grounded after the move are the ones who understand what they are trading — and why. Switching environments doesn't erase stress. It redistributes it.

When nurses move from an ASC into a hospital with realistic expectations, the transition is far less destabilizing. They understand that the system will operate differently and adjust their work accordingly rather than assuming their skills no longer apply. Hospitals run on scale. Decisions move through layers. Problems take longer to resolve. That does not mean the nurse has less value — it means the value shows up differently.

ASC nurses bring strong skills to hospital settings: anticipating problems before they escalate, recognizing how one decision affects the whole unit, and communicating clearly under pressure about what changes are not the skill itself, but where and how it is used. Nurses who struggle often try to force ASC-style speed and control into a hospital system that isn't built for it. Nurses who stabilize learn to use the hospital's structure rather than fight it—documenting thoroughly, escalating intentionally, and allowing the system to carry out what it was designed to carry out. When nurses align how they work with how the system actually functions, the transition stops feeling chaotic and starts feeling sustainable.

WHY SOME NURSES THRIVE —AND OTHERS DON'T

When nurses move between hospitals and ASCs, outcomes vary widely. Some feel immediate relief and stability. Others feel disoriented, depleted, or quietly unhappy. What's important to understand is this: the difference is rarely about skill, intelligence, or work ethic. It is about **alignment**. Hospitals and ASCs reward different traits, regulate stress differently, and exert pressure in various ways. Nurses who thrive are not stronger or more adaptable—they are operating in environments that align with how they process pressure, authority, and uncertainty.

Thriving Is About How Pressure Is Experienced

In hospitals, pressure is constant and diffuse. It comes from patient volume, acuity, staffing shortages, and emotional exposure. The stress is ongoing but shared. When something goes wrong, the system absorbs much of the impact. Nurses who thrive here tend to tolerate sustained intensity. They can compartmentalize. They function well amid noise, interruptions, and competing demands. They can document, escalate, and move on without requiring immediate resolution.

In ASCs, pressure is intermittent but concentrated. The day may feel manageable until it suddenly isn't. When pressure increases, it affects everyone simultaneously, in proximity, with little insulation. Nurses who thrive here tend to regulate themselves quickly. They communicate clearly under stress. They do not take abrupt tone shifts personally. They recover fast from interpersonal friction and return to baseline without rumination. Neither response is better. They are simply different strengths of the nervous system.

Visibility Is a Deciding Factor

Some nurses thrive when they are known. They like being trusted, relied upon, and recognized as integral to the team. They perform well when expectations are clear and relationships are stable. ASCs amplify these traits. Other nurses thrive when visibility is limited. They value privacy, clear role boundaries, and the ability to do their work without interpersonal scrutiny. Hospitals offer this distance through scale. When a nurse who values anonymity enters a high-visibility ASC, she may feel exposed and self-conscious. When a nurse who values recognition enters a large hospital system, she may feel invisible or underutilized. Neither reaction is weakness. It is feedback.

Different Relationships to Authority

Hospitals rely on formal authority. Policies, procedures, and escalation pathways govern decisions. Nurses who are comfortable working within structured hierarchies tend to feel protected in such settings. They trust systems more than personalities. ASCs rely more heavily on informal authority. Influence often flows through relationships, reputation, and consistency rather than titles alone. Nurses who are comfortable navigating nuance and asserting boundaries calmly tend to do better. Nurses struggle when they expect one form of authority in the other system. Hospital-trained nurses may expect policy to override personality in ASCs. ASC nurses may expect decisiveness and flexibility in hospitals that cannot move that fast. Misalignment here creates frustration that feels personal — but isn't.

How Emotional Labor Is Distributed

Hospitals demand emotional endurance. Nurses carry patients longer, witness decline, and manage family dynamics over time. The emotional labor is cumulative. ASCs demand emotional precision. Nurses manage high expectations, fast turnovers, and repeated interactions with the same clinicians. The emotional labor is relational. Nurses who thrive are not those who "feel less." They are those whose emotional strengths match the environment's demands.

Why Competence Is Not the Issue

One of the most damaging misunderstandings nurses have during transitions is the assumption that struggle indicates inadequacy. It doesn't. A nurse can be highly competent and still feel unsettled in an environment that doesn't align with how she processes stress, authority, or visibility. When this misalignment goes unnamed, nurses internalize it as failure. In reality, the environment is asking for a different operating style, not a different level of skill.

The Pattern That Predicts Success

Nurses who thrive after switching environments tend to do one thing consistently: they **adapt how they operate**, not who they are.

They adjust expectations.

They relearn escalation.

They recalibrate boundaries.

They stop assuming familiarity where structure has changed.

Nurses who struggle often try to carry the same operating assumptions into a fundamentally different system. The mismatch creates friction, self-doubt, and fatigue.

What This Section Is Asking You to Consider

This section is not asking nurses to choose the "right" environment forever. It is asking them to recognize what fits *now*. Alignment changes over time. What worked early in a career may not work later. What felt stabilizing once may feel limiting later. Thriving is not about loyalty to a system. It is about honesty with yourself. When nurses stop asking, *"Why can't I handle this?"* and start asking, *"What kind of system supports how I work best right now?"* something important shifts. The work becomes sustainable again — not because the job got easier, but because the environment stopped fighting the nurse. That is the difference between surviving a role and thriving in it.

HOW TO MOVE INTENTIONALLY (NOT REACTIVELY)

Most nurses do not leave hospitals or ASCs because they planned a transition. They leave because something finally became unsustainable.

A breaking point.

A bad stretch that never resolved.

A sense that the environment was eroding them faster than they could recover.

Reactive moves are understandable. They are also risky. Moving intentionally does not mean waiting for perfect conditions. It means understanding what you are walking *into*, not just what you are walking *away from*.

Why Reactive Moves Often Disappoint

When nurses move reactively, they carry unexamined assumptions with them.

Hospital nurses assume an ASC will remove stress entirely. ASC nurses assume a hospital will automatically provide protection. When the new environment fails to meet those assumptions, disappointment feels personal. Nurses

conclude they misjudged themselves or made a mistake —
when in reality, they misjudged the *system*. Intentional moves
begin with recalibration, not escape.

What to Observe Before You Switch

Before accepting a role, nurses often inquire about the schedule, compensation, and benefits. Those matters. They do not
predict sustainability. What matters more is culture under
pressure.

Intentional nurses observe how the environment behaves
on hard days:

- What happens when the schedule runs late?
- How are staffing gaps handled?
- Who makes decisions when there is disagreement?
- How is conflict addressed — or avoided?
- What happens when someone says no?

These moments reveal more than any interview answer. If
you cannot observe directly, ask nurses privately how inconsistency shows up — and whether it is addressed or absorbed.
Ask for a "shadow day." Spend the day, or even a few hours,
observing.

Learning the Informal Power Map

Every healthcare environment has two org charts:

- the one on paper
- the one people actually follow

Intentional nurses learn the second one early.

They notice whose voice carries weight, who is deferred to, and who absorbs friction. They watch how decisions are made when leadership is present — and when it isn't. They pay attention to who enforces standards and who quietly negotiates them away. This is not cynicism. It is situational awareness. Knowing the informal power map allows nurses to navigate without internalizing chaos.

The First 90 Days: Why Less Is More

One of the most common mistakes nurses make during transitions is trying to prove themselves too quickly. Intentional nurses slow down at first.

They listen more than they speak.

They learn patterns before challenging them.

They avoid over-accommodating to "fit in."

They protect their documentation habits.

This is not passivity. It is strategic patience. Early overextension teaches the environment what you will tolerate. Boundaries are easier to establish early than to rebuild later.

Rebuilding Your Internal Operating System

Every environment requires a different internal posture. Hospital nurses moving to ASCs must adjust to visibility, immediacy, and informal influence. ASC nurses moving to hospitals must adapt to bureaucratic processes, delayed resolution, and scale.

Intentional nurses update how they:

- escalate concerns
- interpret tone
- measure success

- define safety
- recover after difficult days

They stop assuming the same behaviors will yield the same results in a different system. Adaptation is not self-betrayal. It is professional intelligence.

Choosing What to Carry Forward—and What to Let Go

Not every habit transfers well. Hospital nurses may need to release the expectation that policy alone will protect them in an ASC. ASC nurses may need to dispel the expectation that speed equates to effectiveness in the hospital setting.

Intentional nurses decide consciously:

- Which skills still serve them
- Which expectations need adjustment
- Which boundaries are non-negotiable

This prevents constant friction between who they are and where they are.

Why This Approach Prevents Regret

Regret after a move often comes from feeling blindsided. Intentional moves reduce surprise. Nurses still encounter difficulties, but they recognize them as structural rather than personal. That recognition preserves confidence and prevents self-doubt from taking over. Instead of asking, *"Why is this happening to me?"* they ask, *"How does this system handle pressure — and how do I operate within it?"* That shift changes everything.

The Core Principle of Intentional Movement

Intentional transitions are not about finding the perfect job. They are about choosing an environment whose stress you understand and can manage *now*. Careers evolve. So do nervous systems. What fits at one stage may not fit at another. Moving intentionally acknowledges that reality rather than fighting it.

Leaving a hospital for an ASC — or an ASC for a hospital — does not reset your career. It repositions it. When nurses move with understanding instead of desperation, the transition becomes stabilizing rather than destabilizing. The environment no longer defines their worth — it simply becomes the context they navigate. That is the difference between reacting to burnout and reclaiming direction.

8

WORKING WITH DOCTORS

WHAT "MANAGING DOCTORS" REALLY MEANS

W hen nurses discuss managing doctors, they are not referring to authority or control. They are discussing preventing the day from falling apart. They are discussing managing the space between what a surgeon wants to do and what the unit can realistically support without compromising quality or burning out staff.

What This Work Really Is

Managing doctors is not about authority. It is about keeping care safe, staff steady, and the day moving without chaos. When this work is done well, no one notices it. When it's missing, everyone feels it. Much of this work begins before anyone speaks. Nurses learn to anticipate preferences because waiting until a surgeon asks usually means you're already behind. Equipment is pulled early. Positioning is adjusted ahead of time. Timing is adjusted so corrections don't have to be made later, when the room is tense, and patience is gone. None of this is written down. It's learned the hard way.

If This Feels Familiar

If you're already setting things up "just in case," Slowing

things down without calling it a delay, or a smoothing tone, so patients don't notice tension. You're already doing this work. Nurses also continually adjust workflows to prevent minor problems from escalating. Breaks get shifted. Tasks get reordered. Someone covers a handoff to prevent a room from stalling. These choices aren't about being nice — they're about keeping the whole place running without unnecessary friction.

Another big part of managing doctors is translation. When a surgeon says, "Let's add one more case," the nurse immediately hears what that actually means on the floor: staffing stretched thin, PACU filling up, anesthesia coverage tightening, and people getting tired. Instead of saying no outright, the nurse reframes the decision in practical terms so it can be made with the whole picture in mind.

What's Really Happening Here

This isn't about attitude. It's about pressure colliding with limits. Seeing that difference helps you respond without taking it personally. That same pressure often shows up as tone. When a surgeon's voice sharpens, or frustration spills into the hallway, nurses step in to contain it. They redirect the moment away from patients. They keep tension from spreading to the desk, the OR, or the PACU. Most patients never realize how close the system is to strain — because nurses are quietly holding that line. De-escalation is part of the job, whether anyone names it or not. Nurses learn to choose their words carefully, when to speak up immediately, and when waiting will actually get the concern addressed. Safety gets protected without making anyone feel challenged.

Navigation vs Absorption

Navigation keeps the day moving.

Absorption wears you down.

WHY THIS ROLE FALLS TO NURSES

Doctors and nurses are trained differently, and that difference matters most on hard days. Surgeons are trained to focus on outcomes, speed, decisiveness, and keeping momentum. Delays feel like problems that need to be pushed through. Nurses are trained to consider the entire shift—not just the case at hand. They're monitoring safety, flow, staffing, recovery, and what happens three steps down the line if something changes now.

Why This Matters

Both perspectives are necessary.

The trouble starts when pressure forces one to override the other. Add time pressure, production demands, hierarchy, reputation, fatigue, and tension, and tension builds quickly. Someone has to catch it before it turns into chaos. Most of the time, that someone is the nurse.

WHEN MANAGING DOCTORS BECOMES A PROBLEM

Managing doctors crosses the line when responsibility is assigned to nurses informally, without authority, support, or protection.

Warning Signs

You find yourself walking on eggshells.

You replay conversations after your shift.

You brace when certain surgeons walk in.

You stop escalating because it doesn't feel safe.

You feel responsible for everyone's mood.

At that point, you're not just doing your job. You're carrying stress that should be shared or addressed at a higher level.

WHAT HEALTHY SYSTEMS DO DIFFERENTLY

Healthier units don't pretend pressure doesn't exist. They deal with it openly. Expectations for behavior are clear. There's a known path for escalation—leadership steps in instead of letting nurses absorb everything.

A Critical Boundary

If keeping things calm means staying silent, over-accommodating, or swallowing frustration, something is off. Doctors still feel pressure. It just doesn't all land on the nurse.

WHAT NURSES CAN CONTROL

Even when the system isn't perfect, nurses still have leverage. They use a steady, neutral tone rather than explaining or apologizing. They escalate through the appropriate channels rather than negotiating one-on-one. They document what happened and what it affected, not how it felt. They learn to notice when they're managing the work — and when they're managing emotions that aren't theirs.

What You Can Control

You can't fix the system alone.

You *can* stop blaming yourself for it. This doesn't make the job easy. It makes it survivable.

WHY NAMING THIS MATTERS

The hardest part of managing doctors isn't the work itself. It's doing it without language or recognition. When no one names it, nurses assume it's just part of being "good."

Why Naming This Changes Everything

What stays unnamed gets internalized. What's named can

be shared and supported. Once this work has a name, it's easier to set limits around it.

Example: Before and After Naming the Work

Before it's named

A nurse stays late again because a surgeon added a case at the end of the day. She rearranged staffing, covered PACU when it backed up, addressed the surgeon's frustration, and ensured patients never felt rushed. No one acknowledged it. No one discussed it. It was just "how the day went." Driving home, she feels drained and slightly resentful, but she tells herself this is just part of being a good nurse. She doesn't mention it to leadership because she doesn't know how to describe what actually happened. All she knows is that she feels worn down — and she assumes that feeling is her problem. The work stays unnamed. So the stress gets internalized.

After it's named

The same situation happens. A surgeon adds a case late. The nurse again manages staffing, flow, tone, and patient experience. But this time, she names what occurred when speaking to leadership: "Adding that case required rearranging staffing, covering PACU overflow, and managing patient expectations. That's manageable occasionally, but it can't be our default."

Now the issue isn't her stamina or attitude. It's a **system decision with consequences**. Leadership can respond. They can decide whether add-ons need limits, approval, or staffing adjustments. The nurse is no longer silently absorbing the cost. The work uses language to enable sharing and support.

Why This Changes Everything

Before naming, the nurse feels:

- tired
- resentful
- unsure if she's being unreasonable

After naming, the nurse feels:

- clear
- grounded
- less alone

She can now set limits without guilt because she's describing reality, not complaining.

ASC SCENARIOS: LANGUAGE FOR REAL-WORLD MOMENTS

In ASCs, conversations occur quickly, publicly, and repeatedly with the same people. Language has to be efficient, neutral, and repeatable. These scripts are designed to hold boundaries without creating friction.

SCENARIO 1: LATE SURGEON ARRIVAL

The reality: Late starts cascade quickly in ASCs. Staff, anesthesia, and PACU absorb the impact.

What not to do: Explain. Apologize excessively. Personalize the delay.

Language to use:

- "We're adjusting the schedule to maintain patient flow and recovery coverage."
- "Here's how we're resetting the day based on current timing."
- "To keep this consistent, we're following the same process we use for late starts."

Why this works: It frames the response as *system-based* rather than punitive or personal.

SCENARIO 2: SURGEON WANTS TO BUMP CASES

The reality: Bumping feels minor to the surgeon and disruptive to everyone else.

Language to use:

- "Bumping would create a recovery bottleneck later today."
- "We can either keep the current order or delay the add-on. Those are the options that fit today's capacity."
- "To keep this fair across surgeons, we're not bumping scheduled cases."

Why this works: It provides structure rather than debate.

SCENARIO 3: ADD-ON CASE PRESSURE

The reality: Add-ons are common, chaos is not.

Language to use:

- "If we add this case, we'll exceed PACU staffing."
- "We can add it today or maintain safe discharge flow. Which should we prioritize?"
- "This would be an exception and won't reset our standard."

Why this works: It separates clinical desire from operational reality.

SCENARIO 4: TURNOVER DELAY BLAME

The reality: Turnovers are a frequent flashpoint.
Language to use:

- "Here's where the delay occurred and what's being addressed."
- "We're aligning to keep the next turnover within expectations."
- "Let's confirm what's needed to move forward."

Why this works: It shifts the conversation from blame to resolution.

PREFERENCE CONFLICTS (SURGEON A VS SURGEON B): WHY THIS BECOMES PERSONAL

An actual preference conflict occurs when **two surgeons want different things**, leaving the nurse in the middle.
Example:

- Surgeon A prefers a specific setup, instrument order, or workflow.
- Surgeon B prefers the opposite.
- Both expect *their* preference to be followed, especially when they're in the room.

Without a standard, the nurse becomes the decision-maker by default. That's where personal negotiation begins.

STOP BEING THE REFEREE

One of the fastest ways nurses burn out in ASCs is by becoming the referee between physicians. It rarely starts intentionally. It begins when two surgeons want different things, there is no clear standard, and someone has to decide on the spot. That "someone" is usually the nurse standing in the room. Over time, nurses stop just setting up cases. They begin to remember who prefers what, who becomes irritated by which detail, and which compromise will cause the least friction today. None of this is written down. None of it is protected. All of this places the nurse in the middle. Being the referee feels like part of being good at the job — until it isn't.

What Being the Referee Actually Looks Like

You know you're acting as the referee when:

- You adjust setups depending on which surgeon is present
- You change how you enforce rules based on who is asking
- You brace for backlash when one surgeon finds out you did it differently for another
- You feel responsible for keeping everyone "even."
- You spend energy defending decisions you were never meant to make

At that point, you're not just managing workflow. You're managing relationships that belong to leadership and policy.

WHAT PERSONAL NEGOTIATION LOOKS LIKE IN THIS SCENARIO

Without standardized language, the interaction often sounds like this:

- Surgeon A: "This is how I like it."
- Nurse: "Okay, we'll do it your way."

Later:

- Surgeon B: "Why is this set up like that?"
- Nurse: "That's how Surgeon A prefers it."

Now the nurse is:

- explaining herself
- defending past decisions
- implicitly choosing sides

From the surgeon's perspective, it feels inconsistent. From the nurse's perspective, it feels like being pulled apart. This is no longer a preference issue. It's a credibility and fairness issue — and the nurse is holding it alone. That is personal negotiation.

HOW THE SCRIPT REMOVES PERSONAL NEGOTIATION IN A TWO-SURGEON CONFLICT

Now let's look at the same situation using the scripted language.

Script 1

"We're standardizing this across surgeons when feasible."

This immediately changes the frame. The nurse is no longer saying:

- "I decided this," or
- "I'm choosing one surgeon over the other."

She's saying:

- "This is not a Surgeon A vs Surgeon B issue."
- "This is a center-wide approach."

The conflict moves out of the nurse's hands and into the system.

Script 2

"This preference falls into our efficiency category, not a safety requirement."

This does something very important in a preference conflict: It explains *why* neither surgeon automatically wins.

Both surgeons now hear:

- "Your preference is valid."
- "It is not mandatory."
- "It is applied when feasible, not guaranteed."

The nurse is no longer negotiating whose preference matters more. She is categorizing the request using a shared framework. Categorization replaces comparison. Comparison creates conflict.

Script 3

"When possible, we accommodate — when not, we follow the standard process."

This closes the loop. Instead of:

- debating whose preference takes priority
- justifying past choices
- adjusting based on who is present

The nurse is signaling:

- predictability
- fairness
- consistency

Both surgeons are treated the same — even if neither gets exactly what they want in that moment.

WHAT EACH SURGEON HEARS (AND WHY IT MATTERS)

Surgeon A no longer hears: "They're favoring Surgeon B." Surgeon B no longer hears: "They always do it Surgeon A's way." Both hear: "This is how the center operates." That shift removes the nurse as the referee.

WHY THIS PROTECTS THE NURSE SPECIFICALLY

In preference conflicts, nurses burn out not from workload, but from **being the negotiator**.

This language:

- removes the need to remember who prefers what *in the moment*
- prevents surgeons from escalating preference battles through the nurse
- reduces resentment toward staff
- protects credibility across the facility

Most importantly, it stops the nurse from becoming the "decider" when she was never given that authority.

PLAIN-LANGUAGE SUMMARY

Personal negotiation sounds like: "I'll do it this way for you."

System consistency sounds like: "Here's how we handle this across surgeons."

In a Surgeon A vs Surgeon B conflict, that difference is everything. It turns a loyalty test into a process.

SCENARIO 6: SHARP TONE OR FRUSTRATION IN THE OR

The reality: Small teams amplify tone.

Language to use:

- "Let's keep this focused on the plan."
- "I want to make sure we stay aligned."
- "Here's where we are operationally."

Why this works: It redirects without confronting.

SCENARIO 7: SAFETY CONCERN THAT MIGHT TRIGGER DEFENSIVENESS

The reality: Speaking up can feel risky in ASCs.

Language to use:

- "Before we proceed, I need to confirm this step."
- "I'm not comfortable moving forward without clarification."
- "Let's pause for safety."

Why this works: It uses direct language without accusation.

SCENARIO 8: LEADERSHIP NOT PRESENT

The reality: Nurses often hold functional authority in the moment.

Language to use:

- "Based on our standard process, here's the plan."
- "This is within my scope to manage."
- "If this needs escalation, I'll involve administration."

Why this works: It establishes authority without over-reaching.

SCENARIO 9: EXCEPTION PRESSURE

The reality: Quiet exceptions destroy consistency.

Language to use:

- "This is an exception due to today's constraints."
- "This does not set a new standard."
- "Next time, we return to the usual process."

Why this works: It prevents precedent creep.

SCENARIO 10: PATIENT OR FAMILY SENSES TENSION

The reality: Patients feel instability immediately.

Language to use:

- "Everything is moving safely and as planned."
- "We're coordinating the next steps."
- "You're in good hands — we'll keep you updated."

Why this works: It protects the patient experience without lying.

THESE SCRIPTS ARE NOT ABOUT CONTROLLING DOCTORS. THEY CONCERN THEMSELVES WITH CONTAINING CHAOS SO THAT CARE CAN PROCEED SAFELY

When nurses use consistent language:

- Decisions feel less personal
- Authority feels predictable
- Escalation becomes safer
- Burnout decreases

QUICK REMINDER

You are not responsible for:

- Managing personalities
- Absorbing frustration
- Fixing systemic issues alone

You are responsible for:

- Clear communication
- Safety
- Professional execution

9

ASC ADMINISTRATION AND EFFECTIVE LEADERSHIP

CONSISTENCY VS INCONSISTENCY

This is not a chapter about management theory. It is about **consistency and causality**.

Chapters 1 through 8 describe what happens when nurses are required to be the most consistent element in fundamentally inconsistent systems. When leadership structures change priorities, expectations, and constraints without stabilizing the environment, nurses are left to absorb the variability. Over time, that mismatch produces predictable outcomes: emotional strain, self-doubt, chronic over-responsibility, erosion of confidence, and, eventually, the realization that something no longer works. Leadership decisions determine whether work is coherent or contradictory. When staffing, scheduling, documentation, escalation, and accountability shift without alignment, inconsistency becomes built into the system. Nurses respond by becoming hyper-consistent—monitoring, compensating, smoothing, anticipating, and holding everything together. What looks like professionalism is often an adaptation to instability. What feels like personal depletion is the cost of carrying coherence in an incoherent structure.

This chapter explains why those patterns repeat across hospitals and ASCs, across units and roles, and across individuals who have never met each other yet arrive at the same conclusion: *I can't keep doing this—not like this.* That conclusion is not burnout speaking. It is clarity emerging. Understanding this does not require anger. It requires accuracy.

When nurses understand that leadership decisions push instability onto staff while keeping decision-making at the top, they stop blaming themselves for problems they were never given the power to fix. They stop blaming themselves for reactions that were rational responses to shifting rules, mixed signals, and uncontained responsibility. And they regain the ability to choose—whether that means redefining how much consistency they will supply, setting firmer boundaries around what they carry, or leaving environments that survive by consuming the steadiness of their nurses without offering structural support in return.

In ASCs, consistency is especially critical because power structures are not always documented in writing. Surgeons may hold financial influence without operational responsibility. Charge nurses may carry functional authority without formal titles. Administrators may be technically in charge while still navigating ownership dynamics, physician preferences, and regulatory demands. If you've ever felt the center run smoothly one week and fracture the next, this is why.

This section of the book focuses on building that consistency from the inside out—not by adding more policies, tightening controls, or demanding more effort from already-stretched teams, but by strengthening the core of your leadership first.

Consistency in an ASC does not begin with procedures or enforcement. It starts with how you think, how you decide, and how you respond under pressure. In fast-moving clinical environments, leaders are constantly tested. Schedules change, personalities clash, unexpected issues arise, and decisions must be made quickly. When leadership responses vary based on stress, urgency, or the people involved, inconsistency becomes the norm—even when intentions are good. Building consistency from the inside out means developing internal steadiness before attempting external control. It requires understanding your default reactions—when you tend to appease, avoid, over-explain, or clamp down—and learning to lead intentionally rather than impulsively. This internal work is invisible, but its effects are not. This is the difference between leadership that stabilizes a center and leadership that unintentionally destabilizes it. Teams quickly sense whether leadership is grounded or reactive, predictable or situational. From there, consistency extends outward into communication. This section will help you refine how you set expectations, deliver decisions, and reinforce standards in ways that reduce uncertainty rather than create resistance. You'll learn how to communicate priorities clearly, respond calmly to pressure, and hold boundaries without escalating conflict — skills that matter in ASCs of every size. Finally, consistency shows up in leadership presence. In ASCs, especially small ones, leadership is always on display. How you enter the building, how you respond when the schedule falls apart, how you handle disagreement — all of it teaches others what to expect. When your presence is steady, the environment stabilizes. When it is unpredictable, anxiety spreads.

===========

In an ASC, inconsistency rarely comes from bad intentions. It shows up in small moments: when a surgeon's request is handled one way on Monday and differently on

Friday; when a nurse asks for guidance and gets a firm answer one day and a vague one the next; when a schedule runs late, and leadership responds with urgency in one situation and silence in another. Individually, these moments seem minor. Collectively, they teach people to stop relying on leadership and start managing uncertainty themselves. Building consistency from the inside out means recognizing those moments and changing how you respond. For example, consider scheduling conflicts. In many ASCs, add-on cases or late starts trigger tension. An inconsistent response might mean accommodating one surgeon immediately, pushing staff to adjust, while telling another surgeon that the schedule is fixed. Over time, nurses learn that "the rules" depend on who is asking. Once that belief sets in, enforcement becomes personal instead of procedural. A consistent leader handles both situations the same way — by referencing shared priorities, explaining the decision, and reinforcing expectations calmly, even when it's uncomfortable.

Consistency also shows up in how issues are addressed. If a nurse raises a concern about turnover safety and the response varies depending on the day or the room's mood, that nurse will stop speaking up. Leaders who build consistency respond predictably: they listen, clarify, and follow up — even if the answer isn't what the nurse hoped for. The predictability matters more than the outcome. Predictability enables staff to continue speaking up rather than retreating. Internal steadiness becomes most visible under pressure. When cases pile up and the day starts unraveling, a reactive leader may rush, snap, or change direction midstream. An avoidant leader may disappear into emails or defer decisions. A steady leader does something different. They pause, identify the priority—patient safety and flow—and make decisions accordingly. Staff don't need perfection in those moments. They need to know what to expect. That expectation becomes the emotional anchor of the entire day.

Consistency is also reflected in how behavior is handled. In a small ASC, one surgeon's frustration or sharp tone can dominate the room. When leadership addresses that behavior one day but ignores it the next, nurses are left to absorb the impact. Consistent leadership means addressing behavior privately and promptly, regardless of volume, seniority, or convenience. That consistency protects staff and stabilizes culture. These are not dramatic leadership moments. They are ordinary ones — repeated daily. And they are where consistency is built or lost. Consistency is not about being inflexible. It's about being reliable. In ASCs of any size, reliability enables people to stop bracing for uncertainty and focus on care. And when that happens, excellence becomes sustainable — not accidental. ASCs do not fail due to a lack of effort. They struggle when consistency is missing. Most administrators step into their role already working at full capacity. They are juggling surgeons, staff, schedules, compliance, budgets, patient experience, and ownership expectations — often all at once. In that environment, it's easy to mistake constant motion for effective leadership. But motion without consistency creates friction, confusion, and quiet burnout across the entire center. Consistency is not a soft skill. In an ASC, it is an operational necessity.

When expectations are unclear, staff fill in the gaps themselves — often inconsistently. When communication is vague, tension between departments increases. When authority is poorly defined, power shifts toward whoever is loudest, most profitable, or most demanding in the moment. Over time, these minor points of confusion compound into cultural instability, staff turnover, surgeon dissatisfaction, and operational inefficiency. The examples below aren't edge cases; they are how inconsistency shows up in real centers every day.

When expectations are unclear, people fill in the gaps themselves

Example:

In a multi-OR ASC, no one has clearly stated who decides when a late surgeon can bump cases. One nurse allows it to keep the peace. Another refuses because it disrupts recovery staffing. A third escalates it to the administrator only when it affects *her* room. Within weeks, surgeons complain that "rules keep changing," while nurses feel blamed for inconsistency they didn't create. No one is acting maliciously — everyone is just improvising in the absence of direction.

When communication is vague, tension between departments increases

Example:

The administration announces that "turnover times need improvement," but doesn't define what "improvement" means or how it will be measured. OR staff push harder to turn rooms quickly. The PACU resists because patients are arriving faster than beds open. Sterile processing is being blamed for delays for which they weren't consulted. Each department believes they're being reasonable. Tension rises because there is no shared understanding.

When authority is poorly defined, power shifts informally

Example:

Officially, the administrator oversees daily operations. In practice, one high-volume surgeon routinely changes the schedule, adds cases, and overrides staff concerns because "this is how we've always done it." Staff know pushing back leads nowhere. Over time, nurses stop escalating issues to leadership and instead wait to see what the surgeon wants before acting. Leadership still exists on paper, but functional authority has shifted elsewhere.

Power gravitates toward whoever is loudest, most profitable, or most demanding.

Example:

Two surgeons request exceptions to start times. One is calm and flexible; the other is loud, persistent, and threatens to take cases elsewhere. Leadership accommodates the louder surgeon repeatedly. Word spreads quickly. Other surgeons escalate their behavior to get the same treatment. Nurses become reluctant to enforce standards because enforcement is perceived as optional and risky. Volume and tone of voice now determine decisions.

Minor inconsistencies compound into cultural instability

Example:

New nurses receive different answers to the same questions depending on who they ask. Policies exist but are enforced selectively. Staff stop trusting that leadership will be consistent, so they create their own "workarounds." Those workarounds conflict. Frustration grows. Communication becomes guarded. The culture shifts from collaboration to self-protection.

Staff turnover increases quietly at first.

Example:

Experienced nurses don't complain loudly. They stop picking up extra shifts. Then they leave for another center with fewer surprises. Leadership is surprised when resignations occur because no one raised major concerns, even though people had already learned that speaking up didn't lead to clarity or change.

Surgeon dissatisfaction follows

Example:

Surgeons begin to complain about inefficiency, delays, or a "lack of professionalism." What they're reacting to is not staff competence — it's inconsistency. Each surgeon is experiencing a different version of how the center operates. Frustration rises because expectations don't align with reality. Without consistency, even reasonable surgeons feel misled.

Operational inefficiency becomes baked in

Example:

Because no one wants conflict, inefficiencies go unaddressed. Cases start late because everyone assumes someone else is handling it. Supplies aren't standardized because preferences aren't enforced. Add-ons create chaos because decision-making is reactive instead of structured. Leadership spends more time firefighting than improving operations.

Why this matters: None of these problems starts with incompetence. They begin with ambiguity. When expectations, communication, and authority are unclear, people do what humans always do under pressure: they adapt locally. Those adaptations conflict. Over time, the system destabilizes — quietly, predictably, and expensively. This is why consistency is not a leadership preference in an ASC. It is a stabilizing force.

Leading with consistency means intentionally reducing uncertainty wherever possible. It means ensuring that people understand not only *what* is expected of them, but *why* decisions are made and *how* authority is exercised. Consistency enables staff to work confidently rather than defensively. It allows surgeons to focus on patient care rather than on negotiating boundaries. It allows administrators to lead proactively rather than constantly putting out fires.

ASC CONSISTENCY & AUTHORITY DIAGNOSTIC CHECKLIST

This checklist is not about blame. It is about pattern recognition. Answer each question honestly based on what *actually happens*, not what policies say.

1. Decision Ownership

- Do staff know who makes the final call when schedules change mid-day?
- When two surgeons request conflicting accommodations, is the decision process predictable?
- Are decisions made consistently, or do they depend on who is asking?
- Can staff explain *why* a decision was made — even if they disagree with it?

Red flag: Different answers from different people to the same scenario.

2. Expectation Consistency

- Are turnover expectations the same for all surgeons?
- Are start-time standards applied evenly?
- Do staff receive the same guidance regardless of who they ask?
- Are "exceptions" rare and explained — or frequent and unspoken?

Red flag: Phrases like "It depends," "That's how Dr. ___ likes it," or "We usually just…"

3. Communication Under Pressure

- When the day runs behind, does leadership communicate priorities clearly?
- Are changes explained briefly and calmly — or announced abruptly?
- Do staff understand what matters most when everything can't be perfect?
- Is follow-up provided after tense or disruptive days?

Red flag: Increased hallway conversations, side texts, or informal venting.

4. Informal Power Signals

- Whom do staff consult before acting when matters become complicated?

- Whose preferences override policies without discussion?
- Are some behaviors tolerated from certain individuals but not others?
- Has leadership ever avoided addressing behavior because of volume, status, or convenience?

Red flag: Staff wait to see how a specific person reacts before proceeding.

5. Staff Adaptation Behaviors

- Are nurses managing personalities instead of workflows?
- Do staff hesitate to escalate issues because outcomes feel unpredictable?
- Have workarounds become standard practice?
- Are experienced staff quieter than they used to be?

Red flag: Competent people disengaging without complaint.

6. Surgeon Experience

- Do surgeons describe the ASC as "inconsistent" or "disorganized"?
- Do different surgeons receive different versions of "how things work"?
- Are complaints focused on reliability rather than skill?
- Are surgeon expectations aligned with operational reality?

Red flag: Surgeons say, "Last time this was allowed."

7. Early Turnover Indicators

- Are staff declining extra shifts more frequently?
- Are experienced nurses leaving without prolonged complaints?
- Are new hires confused about expectations weeks into the role?
- Is recruitment becoming harder despite competitive pay?

Red flag: Quiet exits rather than loud resignations.

8. Leadership Self-Check

- Do you respond differently depending on stress, timing, or who is involved?
- Have you ever delayed a decision to avoid conflict?
- Do you sometimes change direction mid-day without explaining why?
- Do you assume people "just know" what you expect?

Red flag: Your own answers feel inconsistent.

Closing Reminder: ASCs rarely destabilize due to gaps in effort or skill. They destabilize because uncertainty forces people to self-manage. Consistency restores trust. Trust restores performance.

HELPFUL TOOLS FOR MANAGING CONSISTENCY

1. **Scored Assessment Tool** (for diagnosis and prioritization)
2. **Monthly Leadership Consistency Review** (for ongoing course correction)

Both are designed specifically for **ASC's of any size** and are practical to use.

ASC LEADERSHIP CONSISTENCY — SCORED ASSESSMENT TOOL

Purpose:

To identify where inconsistency and authority drift are occurring *before* they result in burnout, turnover, or surgeon dissatisfaction.

How to use:

For each statement, score yourself honestly based on what happens **most of the time**.

- **0 = Rarely / Not true**

- **1 = Sometimes / Inconsistent**
- **2 = Usually / Consistent**
- **3 = Always / Highly consistent**

A. Decision-Making

1. Staff know who makes the final call when schedules change mid-day.
2. Conflicting surgeon requests are handled using the same criteria each time.
3. Decisions are explained briefly and clearly when they affect workflow.
4. Exceptions are rare and explicitly stated as exceptions.

Section Total (0–12): ___

B. Expectations & Standards

1. Turnover expectations are applied consistently across surgeons.
2. Start-time standards are enforced evenly.
3. Staff receive the same guidance regardless of who they ask.
4. "How we do things" matches what is written or stated.

Section Total (0–12): ___

C. Communication Under Pressure

1. Leadership communicates priorities clearly when the day runs behind.
2. Changes are explained calmly rather than announced abruptly.
3. Follow-up occurs after difficult or disruptive days.
4. Staff are not left guessing after major schedule changes.

Section Total (0–12): ___

D. Authority & Power Signals

1. Informal power does not override formal decisions.
2. High-volume or demanding individuals do not receive unspoken privileges.
3. Behavior expectations are enforced regardless of status.
4. Leadership addresses issues directly rather than avoiding discomfort.

Section Total (0–12): ___

E. Staff & Culture Indicators

1. Nurses escalate issues without fear of unpredictable outcomes.
2. Workarounds are addressed, not normalized.
3. Experienced staff remain engaged and vocal.

4. Staff turnover has not increased quietly.

Section Total (0–12): ___

SCORE INTERPRETATION

- **48–60 | Stable & Predictable**
- Leadership consistency is strong. Maintain with regular review.
- **36–47 | Early Drift**
- Inconsistencies exist. Correct now to prevent culture erosion.
- **24–35 | Authority Instability**
- Staff and surgeons are likely compensating for uncertainty. Intervention needed.
- **Below 24 | High Risk**
- Expect burnout, turnover, and dissatisfaction if unaddressed.

STEP-BY-STEP GUIDE TO CREATE AND MAINTAIN CONSISTENCY IN AN ASC

Step 1: Define what "consistency" means in your center

Consistency is not "everyone doing things their own way." It is **predictable standards** applied consistently, even when it's inconvenient.

Defining Consistency: The Three Areas That Stabilize an ASC

Consistency does not mean doing everything the same way regardless of context. It means responding to the *same type of situation* the same way, every time. In ASCs, consistency must be defined deliberately in three areas. When even one of these is left vague, instability spreads quickly.

1. Workflow Consistency

Workflow is where inconsistency becomes visible fastest.

Workflow consistency answers questions like:

- When cases start late, what happens?
- Who decides whether add-ons are accepted?
- How are turnovers prioritized when the day is behind?
- What information must be communicated during handoffs?

Without clear workflow standards, nurses and staff are forced to improvise in real time. One person accelerates turnover to maintain peace. Another slows down to protect safety. A third escalates only when the pressure becomes unbearable. None of these responses is wrong individually — but together they create chaos.

Defining workflow consistency means agreeing on **decision rules**, not just goals.

For example, instead of saying "We need faster turnovers," define:

- What an acceptable turnover looks like
- What conditions justify slowing down
- Who makes the call when tradeoffs exist
- How add-ons are evaluated consistently

When workflow consistency exists, nurses stop guessing. They know how to proceed without negotiating every decision. Surgeons experience predictability. Patient flow stabilizes — not because pressure disappears, but because uncertainty does.

2. Communication Consistency

Communication consistency is about *how* decisions are delivered, not just what the decision is.

Inconsistency in communication often sounds like:

- firm one day, vague the next
- urgent in one situation, silent in another
- over-explained to one person, under-explained to another

Even when the decision itself is reasonable, inconsistent communication creates anxiety. People spend energy interpreting tone instead of executing plans.

Defining communication consistency means deciding:

- How priorities are stated when the day is behind
- How decisions are explained (briefly and fact-based)
- How changes are announced versus discussed
- What language is used under pressure

For example, when schedules change mid-day, consistent communication might always include:

- The priority driving the decision
- What is changing and what is not
- Who is affected
- What happens next

When communication is predictable, resistance drops. People don't need lengthy explanations — they need reliable ones.

3. Behavior Consistency

Behavior is where culture is built or broken.

Behavior consistency answers questions people rarely ask out loud:

- What tone is acceptable under pressure?
- How are concerns raised safely?
- What happens when someone crosses a line?
- Who is protected — and who is not?

Inconsistency here is especially damaging. If a sharp tone is addressed one day but ignored the next, staff learn that behavior standards are optional. If some people are corrected privately while others are never corrected at all, trust erodes.

Defining behavior consistency means making standards explicit:

- Respectful communication is required at all times
- Safety concerns are raised without retaliation
- Problems are addressed directly, not through gossip
- Accountability applies regardless of volume or status

Consistency in the enforcement of behavior creates psychological safety. People stop bracing. Nurses speak up. Surgeons trust the environment. Performance improves because energy is no longer spent managing personalities.

Why These Three Areas Work Together

Workflow, communication, and behavior are interdependent. You cannot stabilize one without the other.

A straightforward workflow without consistent communication feels abrupt.

Clear communication without behavioral standards can feel unsafe.

Behavior standards without workflow rules feel arbitrary.

When all three are defined and consistently reinforced, the ASC begins to feel grounded—even on difficult days. People know how decisions will be made, how information will be shared, and how they will be treated.

That predictability is what allows excellence to become sustainable rather than accidental.

Step 2: Identify the top 3 "instability triggers"

Predictable Pressure Points: Where Inconsistency Takes Hold

Every ASC experiences periods when pressure increases, and decisions must be made quickly. These moments are not random. They are predictable, recurring stress points where inconsistency most often appears — not because people don't care, but because urgency forces reaction.

When these pressure points are left undefined, the center becomes reactive. Decisions shift based on who is present, who is loudest, or who feels most urgent in the moment. Over time, staff learn that rules are flexible, authority is negotiable, and outcomes are unpredictable. That's where chaos begins. Understanding these pressure points allows you to regain control—not by eliminating stress, but by deciding in advance how to handle it.

Late Surgeon Arrivals and Bumped Cases

Late arrivals are one of the most common and destabilizing triggers in an ASC.

When a surgeon arrives late, several questions immediately arise:

- Do their cases move later?
- Are other surgeons' cases bumped?
- Do staff adjust breaks, recovery flow, or staffing?
- Who makes the call — and based on what criteria?

Inconsistent handling sends the message that timing rules depend on who is running late. Nurses may feel pressured to compensate. Surgeons may expect accommodation. Resentment builds quietly.

Consistency here requires defining:

- How late is "late"
- What happens when that threshold is crossed
- Whether cases are bumped or rescheduled
- Who communicates the decision

When expectations are known in advance, urgency loses its power.

Add-Ons and Schedule Compression

Add-ons compress time, energy, and staffing.

Without defined rules, add-ons are often handled

emotionally: accommodated to maintain peace, denied to avoid chaos, or accepted without considering downstream effects. Each inconsistent decision reinforces confusion.

Consistency means agreeing on:

- When add-ons are considered
- What factors must be present (staffing, PACU capacity, anesthesia coverage)
- Who approves them
- What gets deprioritized if they're accepted

This prevents last-minute scrambling and resentment.

Turnover Delays and Blame Shifting. Turnovers are a pressure cooker. When delays occur, people look for a reason. Without consistent expectations, blame shifts quickly — OR blames PACU, PACU blames SPD, SPD blames staffing, staffing blames leadership.

Consistency here requires clarity on:

- Realistic turnover targets
- Acceptable delays
- Communication expectations when delays occur
- Shared responsibility rather than finger-pointing

Defined processes turn blame into problem-solving.

Preference Conflicts (Surgeon A vs Surgeon B)

Preference conflicts are inevitable — and dangerous if unmanaged. When Surgeon A's preference is treated as mandatory, and Surgeon B's as optional, inconsistency becomes visible instantly. Nurses are forced to navigate competing expectations without protection. Over time, preferences become power plays. Consistency means categorizing preferences:

- Safety-critical
- Efficiency-related
- Personal style

Once categorized, preferences are applied consistently rather than emotionally.

Staff Call-Outs and Staffing Gaps

Staffing gaps quickly expose leadership response patterns.

When someone calls out, the questions come fast:

- Who covers?
- Do cases proceed?
- Are expectations adjusted?
- Does leadership step in or delegate?

Inconsistent responses create resentment and burnout. Some days, people stretch unsafely. On other days, cases are canceled without explanation.

Consistency requires predefined responses:

- Minimum safe staffing
- Decision thresholds for cancellations
- Clear communication to surgeons and staff
- Leadership accountability

When staffing plans are predictable, trust increases — even when the outcome isn't ideal.

Why You Must Pick the Top Three: Trying to fix everything at once guarantees nothing changes.

Every ASC has three pressure points that cause disproportionate chaos. These are the moments where inconsistency is most visible and most damaging. When you stabilize these first, everything else becomes easier.

Picking the top three:

- Reduces cognitive load
- Creates early wins
- Builds trust
- Stops the most frequent energy leaks

Consistency doesn't require perfection.
It requires priority.

When you define how pressure will be handled *before* it arrives, the ASC stops reacting — and starts operating.

Step 3: Write the Decision Rules for Pressure Points

This is where consistency ceases to be a value and becomes an operational reality.

Every ASC has pressure points — moments when urgency spikes and decisions must be made quickly. If decision-making rules are not defined *before* those moments occur, people will still make decisions — but they will be driven by emotion, convenience, volume, or fear of conflict. That is how inconsistency takes hold. Decision rules exist to remove guesswork under pressure. They do not eliminate judgment. They *support* it by providing a shared framework for responding when time is limited and emotions are high. For each major trigger in your center—late starts, add-ons, turnover delays, staffing gaps—decision rules address a small set of critical questions. When these questions are answered in advance, people stop negotiating reality in the moment.

Who Decides?

This is the first and most important question — and the one most ASCs leave vague. When pressure hits, people immediately look for authority. If it isn't clearly defined, they will default to whoever is available, loudest, or most influential. That creates uneven outcomes and resentment.

Defining who decides means explicitly stating:

- Who has final authority in that scenario
- Who can recommend but not decide
- Who must be informed after the decision is made

For example, if add-on cases are requested mid-day:

- Does the administrator make the decision?
- The charge nurse?
- The surgeon?
- A combination — and if so, in what order?

When everyone knows who decides, urgency loses its ability to hijack the process.

What Is the Priority Order?

Most conflicts arise when people prioritize different things simultaneously.

One person is focused on patient safety. Another focuses on keeping the schedule on track. Another is worried about staffing fatigue or fairness. All of these priorities matter — but not equally in every situation.

Decision rules force you to define the order explicitly. For example:

1. Patient safety
2. Adequate staffing and recovery capacity
3. Fairness across surgeons
4. Schedule efficiency

When the priority order is known, decisions feel less personal. People may disagree with the outcome, but they understand the reasoning. That understanding reduces resistance.

What Are the Allowable Options?

Under pressure, people often act as if there are only two choices: *force it* or *cancel everything*. Decision rules expand the middle ground.

Allowable options might include:

- Delaying specific cases rather than bumping entire blocks
- Limiting add-ons to certain time windows
- Adjusting staffing expectations temporarily
- Redistributing cases across rooms when possible

By defining allowable options in advance, you reduce improvisation. Nurses and administrators know what tools they're allowed to use — and what they're not expected to invent on the fly.

What Is Non-Negotiable?

Non-negotiables protect safety and integrity.

These are the lines that do not move, regardless of pressure:

- Minimum staffing ratios
- Recovery capacity limits
- Required time-outs or safety checks
- Behavior standards

When non-negotiables are unclear, people bend them quietly to keep things moving. That creates moral distress and burnout. Defining non-negotiables gives staff permission to stop — and leadership backing when they do. What Counts as an Exception — and Who Approves It? Exceptions are inevitable. Quiet exceptions are dangerous.

Decision rules should state:

- What qualifies as a valid exception
- Who approves it
- How it is communicated
- Whether it sets a precedent (usually, it should not)

When exceptions are visible and rare, consistency is

preserved. When exceptions are quiet, they become the new standard.

Administrator vs. Nurse Roles

Administrators should write these rules in short, clear language—not policies or paragraphs. Think checklists, thresholds, and "if–then" guidance. The goal is usability under pressure.

Nurses play a critical role by refining these rules based on daily reality. They know where plans break down, where timelines are unrealistic, and where safety is compromised. When nurses help shape decision rules, compliance increases, and workarounds decrease.

This collaboration is not about control.

It is about shared clarity.

Why This Step Matters More Than Any Other

If decision rules are not explicit, decisions will still be made — but they will default to:

- Emotion ("Just make it work.")
- Volume ("We can't upset this surgeon.")
- Revenue ("We can't cancel cases.")

Those defaults are inconsistent by nature.

Decision rules replace reaction with intention. They give people confidence, reduce conflict, and protect both staff and leadership from constant renegotiation. Consistency does not come from trying harder in the moment.

It arises from deciding in *advance* how pressure will be managed. That is where consistency becomes real.

Step 4: Standardize the Language Used Under Pressure

In ASC, pressure affects how people perceive language.

When stress rises, tone is scrutinized, meaning is inferred, and intent is often misinterpreted. A sentence that would feel neutral on a calm day can sound dismissive, abrupt, or confrontational when the schedule is behind and everyone is stretched thin. That's why inconsistent language produces inconsistent outcomes — even when the decision itself is sound.

Standardizing language is not about scripting people into rigidity. It's about creating **predictable communication** when emotions and urgency are high. Without shared language, people fill in the gaps. A nurse hears urgency and assumes blame. A surgeon hears hesitation and assumes incompetence. A leader hears pushback and assumes resistance. These interpretation games drain energy and escalate tension. Standard language removes ambiguity.

Why Language Matters More Under Stress

In ASCs, decisions are often made quickly, publicly, and under pressure. When different people explain decisions in different ways—or the same person explains them differently depending on mood—the decision itself becomes secondary to its delivery.

For example, compare:

- "We can't do that today."
- "Given staffing and recovery capacity, we're not able to add that case today."

Both statements reach the same outcome. Only one reduces defensiveness. Standard language anchors decisions in shared priorities rather than personal authority.

What Standardized Language Does

When everyone uses the same phrases during high-pressure moments, several things happen at once:

- Decisions feel less personal
- Authority feels consistent rather than situational
- Emotional escalation decreases
- People spend less time interpreting tone and more time executing the plan

This is especially important in small ASCs, where the same people interact repeatedly, and memory is long.

Core Language Categories to Standardize

Instead of inventing responses in the moment, define short phrases that serve specific functions.

Naming the Priority

This prevents argument by clarifying the rationale for the decision.

- "Here's the priority right now: patient safety and flow."
- "Our priority at this point in the day is recovery capacity."

Offering Structured Choice

This avoids power struggles while maintaining boundaries.

- "We can do X now or Y later. Which do you want prioritized?"
- "We have two options within today's limits."

Reinforcing Fairness

This prevents exceptions from becoming precedents.

- "To keep this fair across surgeons, we're applying the same standard."
- "This is how we handle this situation consistently."

Confirming Alignment

This prevents misunderstandings from spreading.

- "Let's confirm the plan, so we're aligned."
- "Before we move forward, here's what we're doing."

Each phrase does a specific job. Together, they create predictability.

How Standard Language Prevents Escalation

Escalation often begins when people feel dismissed, blamed, or overridden. Standard language neutralizes those triggers by focusing on shared priorities instead of personalities.

When a nurse hears the same phrasing every time a schedule compresses, she knows what it means. When a surgeon hears consistent language around add-ons or delays, expectations stabilize. Over time, resistance declines—not because people are forced to comply, but because outcomes are predictable.

This also protects leadership. When decisions are communicated the same way every time, complaints lose traction. There's less room for "Last time this was allowed" because the language itself reinforces consistency.

Implementation: Keep It Simple

Effective standardized language:

- Is short
- Is neutral
- References priorities, not authority
- Is used by everyone consistently

You do not need long explanations. In fact, over-explaining often increases tension. A few steady phrases, used repeatedly, calm the system more than a detailed justification ever will.

Why This Step Works

Standardizing language shifts the ASC from reactive communication to intentional communication. It replaces emotional improvisation with reliability. People stop guessing what a message "really means" and start trusting what it says. This is one of the fastest ways to stabilize an ASC — because it changes behavior immediately, without restructuring schedules or rewriting policies. When communication becomes predictable, the environment becomes safer.

When the environment feels safer, performance naturally improves.

STEP 5: MAKE EXCEPTIONS VISIBLE AND RARE

In ASCs, exceptions do more cultural damage than almost any other leadership behavior—not because they occur, but because of **how** they occur. An exception occurs when the usual process, rule, or standard is not followed. Add-on cases accepted outside the normal window. A late surgeon's block is protected, while others are bumped. Turnover expectations have been relaxed for one room but not for another. These decisions are often made under pressure to keep the day moving. The danger is not flexibility.

The danger is *silence*.

When an exception is made quietly, the system absorbs it as information. No one hears, "This was unusual." What they hear instead is, *"Apparently, this is allowed."* That assumption spreads faster than any written policy ever could.

This is how consistency erodes without anyone consciously deciding to abandon it.

Why Exceptions Are So Disruptive

Exceptions don't just change outcomes — they change expectations.

In a consistent ASC, people understand that there is a standard way decisions are made. In an inconsistent one, people start watching closely for patterns: *Who gets accommodated? When? Under what conditions?* The absence of explanation invites interpretation.

For nurses, quiet exceptions create uncertainty. The next time a similar situation arises, they are left guessing whether they should repeat the accommodation or enforce the standard. Guessing increases anxiety and uneven enforcement.

For surgeons, quiet exceptions create a sense of entitlement. A request that was granted once is remembered as an option going forward, even if leadership intended it to be a one-time decision.

For leadership, quiet exceptions feel efficient in the moment — and expensive later. Each unspoken deviation weakens the credibility of the standard.

What Making Exceptions "Visible" Actually Means:

Visibility does not require a meeting or an announcement. It requires **clear, immediate framing**.

When an exception occurs, it should be named in real time using consistent language:

- "This is an exception due to today's staffing constraints."
- "This does not set a new standard."
- "Next time, we return to the normal process."

Each part of that language serves a purpose. Naming the exception anchors it to circumstances rather than to people. Stating that it does not set a standard prevents expectation drift. Reinforcing the return to baseline protects the future.

This framing preserves consistency even when the rule cannot be followed.

Example: Add-On Case Under Pressure

Consider an ASC in which add-on cases are typically reviewed by the administrator and accepted only if staffing and PACU capacity permit. One afternoon, a surgeon pushes hard for an add-on late in the day. The team is stretched, but leadership agrees to proceed.

If the decision is communicated simply as *"Okay, we'll do it,"* the exception becomes invisible. Next time, the same surgeon—or another—will expect similar accommodations.

A visible exception sounds different:

"We're accepting this add-on today due to an unexpected cancellation earlier and available recovery capacity. This is an exception. Our normal add-on criteria still apply, and we'll return to that process tomorrow."

The outcome is the same. The expectation is not.

Why Quiet Exceptions Become Precedents

Human systems learn through repetition and memory, not policy. People remember events more vividly than written accounts. When an exception is made without explanation, it becomes part of the informal rulebook. Over time, staff begin enforcing different versions of "how things work" based on their personal experiences.

This is why leaders are often surprised when staff say, *"But this was allowed before."* From the staff's perspective, it was. The system taught them that.

Consistency breaks not because rules change — but because **expectations do**.

The Impact on Nurses:

For nurses, quiet exceptions are exhausting. They create a no-win situation. If a nurse repeats the accommodation, she risks being told she shouldn't have. If she enforces the standard, she risks pushback for being "difficult" or "inflexible." Either way, she absorbs stress that should never have been hers to carry. Visible exceptions remove that burden. Nurses know exactly what was unusual, why it happened, and what to do next time. They are no longer responsible for interpreting leadership intent. Clarity protects confidence.

The Impact on Leadership Credibility:

Leaders lose authority not when they make exceptions — but when they make them inconsistently or without explanation. When exceptions are visible and rare, leadership is seen as thoughtful and deliberate. When they are quiet and frequent, leadership appears reactive and unreliable, even if the decisions were well-intentioned.

Consistency is reinforced not by rigidity, but by **containment**. Exceptions that are named, bounded, and returned to baseline do not weaken standards — they strengthen them.

Making Exceptions Rare:

Visibility alone is not enough. Exceptions must also be *rare*. If exceptions occur frequently, that is feedback—not failure. It usually indicates that the underlying standard needs adjustment or that the system is operating beyond its limits. In those cases, the solution is not to add more exceptions but to revisit the rule itself. A consistent ASC treats repeated exceptions as a signal to refine the process, not as proof that the process doesn't matter.

Why This Step Works

Making exceptions visible and rare preserves the integrity of the system under pressure. It prevents informal rule-making, protects nurses from guesswork, and stabilizes expectations across surgeons and staff. Most importantly, it sends a clear message: *standards remain in place, even on difficult days.* That message enables people to stop bracing for unpredictability and start trusting the environment again. Consistency is not about saying no more often. It's about making "yes" meaningful — and contained.

STEP 6: ALIGN SURGEON PREFERENCES INTO CATEGORIES, NOT CHAOS

Surgeon preferences are a regular part of surgical practice. Treating all preferences as equal is not. In many ASCs, preferences accumulate organically over time. One surgeon likes a particular setup. Another prefers a different turnover rhythm. A third insists on a specific order of steps. None of this is unusual. The problem arises when preferences are allowed to exist without structure. When that happens, nurses are forced to arbitrate among competing expectations in real time, and consistency breaks down.

Preferences themselves do not create chaos. It is produced when preferences are unmanaged.

Why Preferences Become a Source of Instability:

When preferences are not categorized, every request feels urgent and equally important. Nurses are left to decide, moment by moment, which requests are mandatory and which are optional. That decision-making burden does not belong at the bedside or in the room — and it produces predictable outcomes:

- Inconsistent enforcement across surgeons
- Perceived favoritism
- Friction between staff and physicians
- Anxiety about "doing it wrong."
- Quiet resentment and burnout

Over time, preferences cease to feel clinical and begin to feel political. Nurses begin to associate certain surgeons with stress, not because of patient complexity, but because expectations are perceived as unpredictable. Consistency requires distinguishing between *what must be done* and *what is preferred*.

The Three Categories That Restore Order

To reduce chaos, preferences must be aligned into clear categories. This framework removes emotion from enforcement and replaces it with shared understanding.

1. True Safety Requirements

These preferences directly affect patient safety, sterility, and regulatory compliance. They are non-negotiable and must be followed at all times.

Examples include:

- Positioning requirements that protect nerves or airways
- Equipment necessary to perform the procedure safely
- Timing requirements tied to anesthesia or medication safety

Because these preferences are safety-based, they are never debated in the moment. Nurses should not have to justify them, and surgeons should not expect variability. Clear categorization here prevents dangerous shortcuts and relieves staff from the pressure to "make it work" under unsafe conditions.

2. Efficiency Preferences

These preferences improve flow or comfort when conditions allow, but they are not safety-critical.

Examples include:

- Preferred room setup sequences
- Case order preferences within a block
- Timing preferences that work best when staffing and recovery capacity support them

These preferences are honored when feasible and adjusted when constraints exist. The key is consistency: the same feasibility criteria apply across surgeons. When efficiency preferences are treated this way, nurses can respond confidently without appearing uncooperative. The decision is no longer personal — it is operational.

3. Personal Style Preferences (Nice-to-Have, Not Guaranteed)

These preferences reflect individual working styles rather than clinical necessity.

Examples include:

- Music preferences
- Lighting preferences beyond clinical need
- Favored communication styles or routines

Acknowledging these preferences respectfully matters. Guaranteeing them does not. When personal style preferences are treated as optional rather than expected, staff are protected from unrealistic demands, and fairness is preserved.

Why Categorization Reduces Conflict

Categorization does the work that nurses should never have to do themselves. Rather than deciding whose preference matters more, nurses apply the same framework consistently. Instead of negotiating in the moment, administrators can reference agreed-upon categories. Instead of interpreting tone or urgency, staff rely on structure. This eliminates favoritism — real or perceived. Surgeons experience consistency because expectations are applied evenly. Staff experience relief because decision-making is no longer personal. Fairness becomes visible.

Documenting Preferences Without Creating Rigidity

Preferences should be documented in a shared, accessible location, organized by category rather than by individual. This prevents preference lists from becoming overwhelming or outdated.

Documentation should be:

- Concise
- Standardized
- Reviewed periodically
- Aligned with the three-category framework

Nurses play a critical role here by clarifying which preferences fall into which category based on daily workflow realities. Administrators ensure alignment and resolve conflicts when preferences collide. Documentation is not about control. It is about predictability.

Example: Preference Conflict in Practice:

Two surgeons request different turnover sequences. One expects immediate room turnover regardless of PACU flow. The other prefers waiting until recovery beds are confirmed. Without categorization, nurses are forced to choose. With categorization, the response is clear: turnover timing is an efficiency preference governed by recovery capacity. The same criteria apply to both surgeons. The outcome may not satisfy everyone — but it is consistent. That consistency reduces friction far more effectively than accommodation ever could.

Why This Step Works

Aligning preferences into categories transforms preference management from emotional labor into operational clarity. It protects nurses from impossible expectations, prevents escalation between surgeons, and reinforces leadership credibility. Most importantly, it restores the idea that standards — not personalities — guide decisions.

Preferences remain respected. Chaos does not. Consistency is not about eliminating individuality.

It is about ensuring individuality does not destabilize the system. That distinction enables an ASC to operate smoothly, fairly, and sustainably.

STEP 7: CREATE A SIMPLE HANDOFF AND ESCALATION PATHWAY

In ASCs, silence is rarely a sign that everything is fine. More often, it signals that escalation feels unsafe. Nurses do not stop speaking up because they stop caring. They stop speaking up because experience teaches them that escalation is unpredictable. Sometimes it leads to support. Sometimes it leads to scrutiny, dismissal, or quiet retaliation. When outcomes are inconsistent, hesitation becomes a form of self-protection.

This is why inconsistent escalation is one of the most dangerous forms of inconsistency in an ASC.

Why Escalation Breaks Down

Escalation is supposed to be a safety mechanism. In practice, it often becomes a risk calculation.

When nurses are unsure:

- Who to involve,
- When to involve them,
- How concerns will be received,
- Or whether raising an issue will create more problems than it solves,

They delay. They work around the issue. They try to fix it quietly. By the time escalation occurs, the situation is already tense, emotional, or unsafe. This pattern is not a failure of courage.

It is a failure of structure. A clear escalation pathway removes judgment from the moment. It replaces fear with predictability.

What a Clear Escalation Pathway Does

A well-defined pathway answers four questions *before* pressure hits:

1. What nurses are expected to handle independently
2. When administrator or charge involvement is required
3. When surgeon involvement is appropriate
4. What triggers an immediate stop for safety

When these boundaries are explicit, nurses no longer have to guess whether escalation is "too much" or "not enough." They know exactly where responsibility shifts — and where support begins. Predictable escalation protects patients, staff, and leadership simultaneously.

What Nurses Handle Independently

Nurses should be empowered to manage routine workflow decisions within clearly defined parameters. These include:

- Standard turnover execution
- Routine handoffs
- Preference application within established categories
- Communication of expected delays using standardized language

Defining this scope prevents unnecessary escalation and reinforces professional autonomy. Nurses are not deferring responsibility; they are operating within agreed-upon authority. When this scope is unclear, nurses either escalate everything (creating frustration) or escalate nothing (creating risk).

What Requires Administrator or Charge Involvement

Administrator or charge involvement should be required when decisions affect fairness, staffing limits, or operational integrity.

Examples include:

- Schedule compression that impacts multiple rooms
- Staffing gaps that affect safe coverage
- Add-on requests outside the defined criteria
- Repeated workflow breakdowns that exceed routine adjustment

Clear thresholds here prevent nurses from being compelled to make political decisions. They are no longer deciding *whether* to escalate; they are following the established pathway. Leadership presence at these moments signals support, not surveillance.

What Requires Surgeon Involvement

Surgeon involvement should be intentional, not automatic. Surgeons should be engaged when:

- Clinical decisions require their input
- Procedural changes affect patient safety
- Case sequencing impacts outcomes
- Consent or scope of practice questions arise

Surgeons should not be the default point of escalation for operational strain. When nurses escalate operational issues directly to surgeons, it often creates pressure to override standards rather than resolve the system problem. A clear pathway protects surgeons from being drawn into conflicts they shouldn't have to manage — and protects nurses from being pressured to negotiate boundaries on their own.

What Triggers an Immediate Stop for Safety

This is the most critical part of the pathway—and the most often assumed rather than defined.

Immediate stop conditions must be explicit. These may include:

- Staffing below minimum safe levels
- Compromised sterility or equipment failure

- Patient instability beyond procedural tolerance
- Missing critical information or verification

When stop conditions are defined, nurses do not need permission to pause. They have authority. Leadership backs that authority consistently. If stop conditions are vague, nurses hesitate — and hesitation under pressure is dangerous.

Why Clear Escalation Restores Speaking Up

When escalation is predictable, it ceases to be personal.
Nurses no longer have to weigh:

- "Will I be seen as difficult?"
- "Will this come back on me?"
- "Is this worth the risk?"

They follow the pathway. Leadership responds. The system holds. Over time, nurses escalate earlier. Issues are addressed before they escalate emotionally. Safety improves not because people are braver, but because the structure supports them.

How to Communicate the Pathway

A pathway only works if it is known and reinforced.
It should be:

- Written simply
- Communicated verbally
- Referenced during pressure
- Reviewed periodically

Most importantly, leadership must respond consistently when the pathway is used. If escalation is met with annoyance or unpredictability, trust collapses quickly. A predictable response makes escalation safe.

Why This Step Works

A clear handoff and escalation pathway reduces ambiguity during the most vulnerable moments of the day. It protects nurses from isolation, leaders from surprise crises, and patients from preventable risk. Consistency in escalation does not slow operations. It stabilizes them. When nurses know precisely when and how to escalate — and trust the response — they stop working around the system and start working *with* it. That is how speaking up becomes normal again, not heroic.

Step 8: Reinforce behavior standards the same way every time

Behavior inconsistency creates fear and resentment.
Set minimum behavioral standards:

- Respectful tone in clinical spaces
- No public shaming
- No retaliation for safety concerns
- Direct communication vs. sarcasm or intimidation

Addressing Behavior: Why Consistency Matters More Than Severity

Behavior is one of the most potent signals of leadership consistency — and one of the most fragile. In an ASC, how behavior is handled tells staff whether standards are objective or optional. It is not the severity of a response that builds trust. It is the **predictability** of it. When behavior is addressed privately, promptly, and consistently, people feel protected. When it is addressed selectively — or only when it becomes inconvenient — trust erodes quickly.

Why Behavior Must Be Addressed Privately

Public correction creates fear, not accountability.

When behavior is publicly challenged — especially in clinical settings—it shifts the focus from improvement to self-protection. Staff become quieter, more guarded, and less willing to speak up. Surgeons become defensive rather than reflective. The room remembers the embarrassment long after it forgets the lesson.

Private conversations preserve dignity while still rein-forcing standards. They allow leaders to be direct without escalating tension. They also prevent the correction itself from becoming a spectacle that destabilizes the team. Privacy communicates professionalism. It says, *"We address issues, but we don't humiliate people."*

Why Promptness Matters:

Delayed correction sends the wrong message.

When problematic behavior is ignored in the moment and addressed days later — or not at all — staff assume it is toler-ated. The longer the delay, the more the behavior appears sanctioned. By the time leadership intervenes, frustration has already spread. Prompt response does not mean interrupting a case or escalating unnecessarily. It means addressing the issue as soon as it is appropriate and safe to do so. Timing matters, but avoidance is not the same as timing. Consistency requires that behavior be addressed close enough to the event that the connection is clear.

Why Consistency Is Non-Negotiable:

Inconsistent enforcement is more damaging than no enforcement.

When one person's sharp tone is addressed but another's is ignored, staff do not interpret that as nuance. They interpret it as favoritism or fear. Over time, they stop trusting leadership to protect them evenly. Consistency does not mean identical conversations. It means the **same standards** apply regardless of:

- Seniority
- Volume
- Personality
- Convenience

When behavior standards are enforced unevenly, people stop reporting concerns and start absorbing them. That absorption turns into resentment, disengagement, and burnout. Trust collapses not because standards are too strict, but because they are unreliable. The Administrator's Role: Steady, Predictable Enforcement: Administrators set the tone for behavioral consistency through their response pattern. Addressing behavior privately, promptly, and consistently means:

- Naming what occurred without accusation
- Referencing the standard, not personal opinion

- Explaining impact without emotional escalation
- Reinforcing expectations clearly

For example, rather than addressing behavior only when complaints pile up, consistent leaders address it the first time — calmly and directly. This prevents patterns from forming and signals that standards are active rather than symbolic. Leadership credibility is built in these quiet moments.

The Nurse's Role: Neutral Facts and Clear Impact

Nurses play a critical role in maintaining behavioral standards — but only when reporting feels safe and worthwhile.

Reporting behavior using neutral facts means describing:

- What was said or done
- Where and when it occurred
- Who was present

Reporting impact means explaining how the behavior affected:

- Patient safety
- Workflow
- Team communication
- Willingness to speak up

This approach removes interpretation and emotion from the report. It shifts the focus from personality to professionalism.

For example, *"The surgeon raised his voice during turnover and said 'hurry up' in front of the patient, which caused the nurse to hesitate during verification,"* is far more effective than *"He was rude again."*

Neutral reporting allows leadership to act without defensiveness or debate.

What Happens When Behavior Is Enforced Only When Convenient

When behavior is addressed only after it becomes disruptive — or only when leadership feels comfortable — staff learn an unspoken rule: *standards are conditional*. Conditional standards create fear. Fear silences reporting. Silence allows behavior to worsen. By the time leadership intervenes, the damage is already done. This cycle is not caused by weak leadership. It is caused by inconsistent leadership. Consistency breaks the cycle early.

Why This Works

Consistent enforcement of behavior does not create tension. It reduces it.

When people trust that leadership will respond predictably, they stop bracing. Nurses speak up earlier. Surgeons adjust sooner. Issues remain small rather than becoming cultural fractures. Behavior standards are not about control.

They are about safety, dignity, and trust. In a consistent ASC, people know where the lines are — and that those lines will be held calmly, reasonably, and every time. That reliability enables teams to function under pressure without fracturing.

Step 9: Build a "weekly consistency huddle" (10 minutes)

This prevents drift.

Once a week (or every two weeks), review:

- One moment, the center felt smooth
- One moment, it felt unstable
- What rule or expectation needs tightening

Small centers (1–2 OR): This can serve as a brief check-in with the nurse(s).

Large centers: include charge, OR, PACU, sterile processing.

Consistency is maintained through review, not memory.

Step 10: Track 3 stability metrics (simple, not bureaucratic)

Use metrics that reflect consistency, not just productivity:

Examples:

- The number of same-day schedule changes due to unclear authority
- The number of turnover delays caused by unclear responsibility
- The number of repeated complaints about "different rules."
- Nurse retention signals (declining extra shifts, disengagement)

You're watching for drift, not perfection.

Step 11: Repair quickly when an inconsistency happens

Consistency isn't making mistakes. It's repairing fast.

After a chaotic day, do a short repair:

- "Yesterday wasn't handled consistently. Here's what we will do next time."
- "Here is the decision rule going forward."
- "Here is who decides."

Repairing restores trust more quickly than an apology alone.

Step 12: Make consistency a leadership identity, not a project

The final step is the culture shift: Consistency is not a policy rollout.

It's a leadership posture.

When people believe decisions will be predictable and fair:

- Anxiety drops
- Conflict decreases
- Performance rises
- Retention improves

That is what makes excellence sustainable.

QUICK ROLE-SPECIFIC NOTES

For Nurses

Your role in consistency is to:

- Ask for decision rules instead of guessing
- Use standardized phrases under pressure
- Document neutrally when reality needs preserving
- Escalate through the defined path consistently

Your power is in predictable execution and clean communication.

For Administrators

Your role is to:

- Define the decision rules and enforce them evenly
- Make exceptions rare and visible
- Address behavior consistently regardless of status
- Communicate priorities calmly under pressure

Your power is in a predictable leadership presence.

CONCLUSION

CHOOSING WHAT COMES NEXT

If this book has done its job, it has not given you answers so much as it has given you permission.

Permission to acknowledge what the work has cost you.

Permission to name burnout without shame.

Permission to recognize that wanting something different does not mean you chose wrong in the first place.

Nursing requires skill, presence, and emotional steadiness in environments that are rarely steady. Over time, it is natural to reassess how much of yourself you can continue to give—and in what ways. That reassessment is not a failure. It is professional maturity. Some nurses will stay at the bedside and find new ways to protect their energy. Some will move from hospitals to ASCs and discover a better rhythm. Others will step into education, quality, coordination, or entirely different roles where their experience still matters—just in a different form.

There is no single correct path forward. What matters is that your next decision is intentional rather than reactive, informed rather than rushed. You deserve work that respects your limits as much as it values your competence. You are not defined by the role you leave or the one you choose next. You are defined by your ability to listen to yourself and respond with honesty. Whatever you decide, let it be a choice that allows you to remain whole. That, too, is good nursing.

www.ingramcontent.com/pod-product-compliance
Lightning Source LLC
Chambersburg PA
CBHW031846200326
41597CB00012B/296